Improving School Board Effectiveness

Improving School Board Effectiveness

A Balanced Governance Approach

Thomas L. Alsbury
Phil Gore

Editors

Harvard Education Press
Cambridge, Massachusetts

Library of Congress Control Number 2015938616

Paperback ISBN 978-1-61250-876-4
Library Edition ISBN 978-1-61250-877-1

Published by Harvard Education Press,
an imprint of the Harvard Education Publishing Group

Harvard Education Press
8 Story Street
Cambridge, MA 02138

Cover Design: Ciano Design
Cover Image: Spiderstock/E+/Getty Images
The typefaces used in this book are Janson Text and Myriad Pro.

CONTENTS

FOREWORD

Given the right conditions *all* students can learn, just not all at the same pace or in the same way. Maximizing all students' learning potential requires committed attention throughout the education system, from the classroom to the principal's office to the district boardroom. But while much has been written about what makes an effective teacher or school administrator, the roles, responsibilities, and best practices necessary for school boards to contribute to the academic success of students have not received the attention they deserve.

Improving School Board Effectiveness addresses this problem head-on, with personal experience as well as comprehensive, in-depth research. The all-star team of contributors that Thomas Alsbury and Phil Gore have brought together has created a must-read for anyone interested in the complex challenges school boards face, especially regarding the question of how board members can contribute to the central goal of improving student outcomes. Reading this book, past board members can review their experiences and perhaps gain a new perspective on the issues they were called on to address. Current members can examine their roles in the light of the most recent analysis of what makes an effective school board, and, critically, of how to get from where they are now to where they would like to be. And prospective candidates can gain valuable insight into the problems and opportunities that lie ahead.

The relevance of this book extends beyond the boardroom as well. District superintendents, their cabinet members, and other district administrators will find useful information and practical guidance in every chapter as they seek to work more collaboratively with their school boards. Indeed, anyone with an interest in school governance can profit from its pages. But as its title indicates, the focus of *Improving School Board Effectiveness* remains squarely on local school boards and how their members can use current research into proven and promising practices to influence student achievement in their district.

Best practices based on quality research in the area of school board leadership have historically been difficult to find, assess, and apply. Now, the contributors to this book have provided this much-needed information. More specifically, the collection provides both guidance and opportunities for "internal dialogues" and self-reflection regarding a school board's policy role versus its operational role; and the book does so engagingly—not with generic "solutions" but with focused questions and detailed self-assessment tools. I think that's an important distinction because, as I remind my audiences and the leadership of the schools and districts that I work with: "Every school district has its own DNA. One size does not fit all."

Because a single formula for success does not—and could not—exist, the book wisely presents itself as a guidebook, not as a "how-to" maintenance manual. Every preK–12 district in America needs a vertically aligned vision and top-down support—from the boardroom to the classroom—to realize the shared goal of more effective instruction that results in higher achievement and greater learning for *all* students.

Two recent publications have clearly documented the school board's important role in implementing this vision. The first is Shober and Hartney's *Does School Board Leadership Matter?*, a research study conducted under the sponsorship of the Fordham Foundation. It states:

> A district's success in "beating the odds" academically is related to board members' focus on the improvement of academics. Unfortunately, not all board members have this focus; some prefer a gentler approach: developing the "whole child," not placing unreasonable academic expectations on schools, and celebrating the work of educators in the face of external accountability pressures. Nothing is wrong with those other priorities—but they ought not displace the primary goal of presidents, governors, employers, myriad education reformers, and a great many parents in twenty-first-century America: boosting children's learning.[1]

The importance of a school board's role in improving student performance was also a central finding in a publication based on the International Center for Leadership in Education's extensive long-term association with many of the nation's most rapidly improving schools. This work details the importance of a systemwide approach in schools that have made substantial increases in student achievement. Central findings include:

- **It takes a system, not just a teacher:** Research supports what most of us see as common sense: what goes on between the teacher and each student is central to high-level learning. Effective teaching is not the end goal, but a means *to* the end: improved student achievement.
- **All teaching is more effective when effectively supported.** Achieving the goal of improving instruction requires a supportive and aligned system. Stated another way, although effective teaching is essential, it is not sufficient to maximize learning and achievement for all students. An organization-wide commitment is at the heart of improving student learning.[2]

To accomplish these objectives, a district needs an aligned system comprised of three major elements. The first is teaching, which is closest to the students and therefore the most critical of the three. Next is instructional leadership from school and other administrators who directly support the classroom teachers. And finally, there is a need for organizational leadership that is aligned with but more operational than the instructional leadership. Organizational leadership must be directly linked to those at the highest level of authority, and, importantly, it must be supported by the district's school board.

The school board, in turn, needs to create policies and practices that focus its mission on student learning while supporting the educational system at every level. *Improving School Board Effectiveness* lays out strategies for school boards to help their districts in this critical mission. In particular, current and prospective board members can use the valuable advice of the various chapter authors to think about how to achieve the following goals:

- Creating a culture of high academic expectations and positive relationships. *What are the implications for school board members?*
- Establishing a shared vision and communicating it to all constituent groups. *What should the school board's role be?*

- Aligning organizational structures and systems to the vision.
  How can the school board help align district structures/systems to the vision and monitor the results?
- Aligning teacher/leader selection, support, and evaluation.
  What influences on staffing issues should school board members exert and share?
- Supporting decision making with relevant data systems.
  How can data enhance the work and responsibilities of the school board?

This book offers practical tools and proven practices aimed at realizing these goals, as well as opportunities for board members—individually and collaboratively—to reflect on their attitudes, assess their strengths, and define the issues they need to address.

Thank you to Thomas Alsbury and Phil Gore for compiling this very worthwhile and instructive book. And to all school board members, thank you for your ongoing commitment to our schools and our children.

Willard R. Daggett, Ed.D.
Founder and Chairman,
International Center for Leadership in Education

PART I

Research Supporting a Balanced Governance Approach

INTRODUCTION

A Call for Balanced Governance

Thomas L. Alsbury

Over the past decade school districts have been under increased pressure to address and improve student achievement, especially for those students who have traditionally performed poorly on academic assessments. State and national reform efforts initially focused on improving teacher quality, but recently the focus has shifted to the possible effect of school leadership on student achievement. The attention turned first to building-level principals and superintendents, but now questions have been raised on whether school boards can influence improvements in school academic performance. The initial discussion must include two questions, the first being whether school boards *should* get involved in these matters, or whether they should be left entirely to the school administration and personnel. And if the board determines that they should get involved, the next question is *how* that should be accomplished. Even if one agrees that improving student achievement is a worthwhile goal, it is reasonable to ask whether school boards actually have this capacity.

DO SCHOOL BOARDS MATTER?

Current research makes it clear that school boards do indeed make a difference in student achievement. Undeniably, increases and declines in student performance link to board member values and beliefs,[1] actions,[2] teamwork,[3] and political conflict and turnover.[4] Previous studies provide evidence that beliefs influence board member actions at the board table and that those decisions influence the beliefs in the system and affect school culture. When the structures and norms of behavior within the school culture positively affect instructional practices, improved student achievement is expected and typical. Recent compilations of school board research are few and focus mainly on empirical studies that support the use of elected school boards,[5] or focus on the presumed failure of elected boards.[6] Nancy Walser provides some evidence of effective school boards for student achievement through case study review.[7]

Even school board critics suggest that boards can harm student performance and thus agree that they do exercise influence. A recent study conducted by the Thomas B. Fordham Institute concluded, "The fact that board members can influence achievement, even loosely, merits much more attention—surely by scholars but also by voters, parents, taxpayers, and other policy-makers."[8] This is a particularly significant conclusion considering that Chester Finn—president of the Fordham Institute and former assistant secretary of the U.S. Department of Education—has asserted, "The local school board, especially the elected kind, is an anachronism and an outrage . . . We need to steel ourselves to put this dysfunctional arrangement out of its misery and move on to something that will work for children."[9]

It appears that both supporters and opponents of elected school boards seem to agree: school boards do indeed affect the schools they govern. This answers the first of our two critical questions. If board members on elected school boards do make a difference, then the next broad question is *how* that difference is actually made.

HOW BOARD MEMBERS MAKE A DIFFERENCE

Models of school board governance and the resulting training received by school boards nationally tend to favor one of two extremes regarding the purpose of school boards. On the one extreme, boards are viewed as political entities whose only task is to provide a communication loop between the school district and the public. As such, board members would not be encouraged to engage in conversations or actions around student achievement or instructional improvement. At best, the board would hire an effective superintendent and get out of his or her way.

The other end of the spectrum regarding board purpose would call on board members to participate in every facet of the school. This harks back to the traditional role of board members who would be assigned to a single school and provide all leadership, including hiring the teacher and cleaning the building. This position is traditionally reinforced by most state laws that give school boards authority over virtually all facets of decision making in a school.

The editors and contributors to this book take the position that school boards can and do make a positive difference in the performance of school personnel and consequently in student achievement. How board members might set about accomplishing this task would seem, on the surface, to be a relatively straightforward question. Traditionally, this would include hiring the superintendent, approving budgets developed by the school staff, approving policy written by school leaders, and influencing the local community to support the passage of bonds and levies. However, defining the *effectiveness* of board service is not always as clear a matter. As described below and in the following chapters, this book focuses on how particular board beliefs and actions can positively influence student achievement. First, however, we should take a brief look at the structure, role, and function of local school boards in the American education system.

Board Structure

There is a fundamental question concerning whether the governance structure itself makes a difference in student improvement. In the United States, state law determines the make-up of most school boards, but there is variety among board structures. Namely, some boards are citywide and some countywide, some board members are elected and some are appointed, some districts are governed by mayors and some by appointed and/or elected councils connected to city or county government, while other boards are hybrid models of the above. The issue of whether schools should be governed by a centralized or a local entity is under debate and is contested.[10]

Board Role

Another way to define school board effectiveness is in the role that boards play. Currently, some governance models suggest a wide spectrum for how board members are to be involved. Specifically, some governance models call for the school board to hire an effective superintendent as a CEO and then adopt a role of monitoring measureable outcomes. Governance models on the other end of the spectrum, buoyed by the legal authority of school boards in most states, call for board members to exercise scrutiny of the finest details of operations and management. School board members are left with the challenge of determining which of these governance approaches is best suited to improving student achievement in their district.

Board Function

One additional issue (although not the final one) is the question of how board beliefs, values, and actions might support improved student achievement. As examples, a board member's actions could positively or negatively influence the superintendent, a fellow board member, and teamwork among the entire board, the community, school district administrators, or school district personnel. Hence, board members are left with the question of how they should act in a variety of settings and with a variety of stakeholders (e.g., at the board meeting, community events, the school, and with the staff).

BALANCED GOVERNANCE: A NEW MODEL FOR SCHOOL BOARD EFFECTIVENESS

While not all questions regarding these three broad governance topics can be answered in a single book, the chapters that follow address some of these issues and provide concrete tools that can be used to improve the performance of school board members. In examining all three topics (structure, role, function), we are introducing a new model of school board governance called Balanced Governance—a model that recognizes that the most effective approach to school board work is through *balance*, avoiding extremes in structure, role, and function.

Given the pressure to improve student outcomes on everything from content knowledge to skills identified as necessary for career and college success, school boards cannot be passive actors. Neither can they replace the specialized knowledge of superintendents and administrators trained in the complex matters of running school districts. However, boards that leverage their own expertise as engaged and knowledgeable representatives of their communities can play a critical role in increasing student achievement. As shown in figure I.1, the Balanced Governance model seeks a middle ground between overly centralized and overly decentralized control on the part of the school board. In particular, it differs from the dominant governance model established in the Progressive Era and other centralized models being promoted by various political constituencies in the United States.

Proponents of eliminating local governance of schools point to the success on international test results of countries with more centralized governance. However, recent evidence indicates that these governance systems often result in unintended shortcomings, leading some international policy makers to call for a more Balanced Governance–style approach. They are looking at the U.S. system of locally elected school boards in combination with central governing boards. The 2012 report of the Program for International Student Achievement (PISA) test results indicates that "school systems that grant more autonomy to schools to define and elaborate their curriculum and assessments perform better than systems that don't," and that there is "a positive correlation in school autonomy for resource allocation and improved student performance."[11]

Balanced Governance: Effective School Board Structure

Over the last century, governance reform attempted to address a purported lack of effectiveness of elected school boards by instituting more professionalized management of America's school systems. One reform replaces elected school boards with mayoral takeover or city appointment of school boards—both forms of centralized governance. Those supporting centralized governance argue that this approach removes the "din" of multiple stakeholder voices, diminishes competing interests,

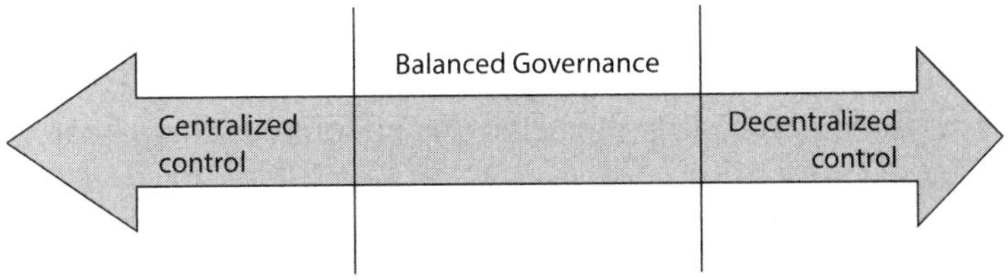

Figure I.1 Balanced Governance: The school board structure

and allows for a more efficient operation of school districts by consolidating decision making in a single leader.[12]

Supporters of locally elected school board governance often challenge these arguments, favoring the expansion of voices in the process of school governance. Critics of centralized governance argue that while mayoral-appointed boards may be more efficient, they reduce democratic participation in school governance. Centralized governance increases politics and competition over scarce resources, as city-council-controlled school systems use education funds in their budgets to enhance social services outside of education. In addition, centralized governance diminishes access to the democratic process by local citizens. Locally elected citizens no longer run their schools, and local community board meetings no longer provide opportunities for community input and influence.

We are, for perhaps the first time in American history, faced with local, state, and federal leaders seriously considering the elimination of a key component of the wider purpose of democratic education—in other words, with the demise of what has been described as the "the crucible of democracy."[13] Researchers have long debated whether governance through elected school boards is democratic, with some suggesting that elected boards often are not responsive to citizen demands, while others note that citizens have the liberty to take action to change schools, and in fact do so when they feel the need.[14]

The decision for local governance of schools was not taken lightly by the framers of the Constitution, who debated for over half a decade as to not only what the purpose of schools in America should be, but also who should have power over what children would learn and be able to do. It was Thomas Jefferson who swayed his counterparts to cede the power of educational decisions and policy to the local community.[15] He stated that with every changing federal administration would come a shift to the curriculum based solely on political agendas, rather than on the welfare of children and a future America. It is crucial to continue to question the underlying political, economic, and sociological factors driving centralized education governance, including the belief that appointed school boards can act as vehicles for patronage politics.

In the end, when assessing the various viewpoints and interests expressed in the governance debate, one must keep in mind that traditionally elected school boards in highly complex urban settings may need assistance in fulfilling their obligations to the students. One solution is to improve the effectiveness of the existing board through a Balanced Governance approach to training and assessment. This is the primary purpose for the tools and recommendations set forth in this book.

Balanced Governance: School Board Role and Function

The focus of this book is the improvement of locally elected school boards. The chapters that follow provide tools and promising practices of highly effective school boards that best support improved student achievement. One overarching ideal is that highly effective boards, both in the United States and internationally, tend to avoid governance extremes. This prompted a new vision of the *board's role* in student achievement through the introduction of the Balanced Governance model. The concept of Balanced Governance provides the overall framework for this book. The research findings and effective practices highlighted here build the case for a new model of local governance that balances the authority of a superintendent to lead a school district, with the necessary oversight of a locally engaged and knowledgeable board.

Balanced Governance is not a single prescribed model or program, but describes a school governance approach that supports and promotes "balance"— discouraging micromanaging on one end of the governance continuum and a disengaged, rubber-stamping board on the other. A board is practicing Balanced Governance if it generally operates within the range shown in figure I.2.

Figure I.2 Balanced Governance: The school board member role

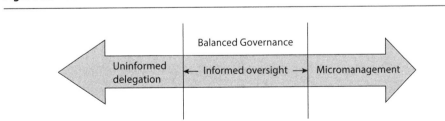

As depicted, a disengaged board is one that believes that they are not able to understand the complexities of the educational system and serve only to approve and support policy directives and communicate those to the public. As a result, the board takes on the role of uninformed delegation. Specifically, the board members and superintendent believe that the board is most effective when it avoids meddling in the processes or means of the district and delegates all responsibility to the superintendent. In this approach to district governance, the boards may set outcome goals for academic achievement on a particular measure, but do not understand the specific gaps or deficits among the students. They also do not understand the programs being used to achieve improvements—neither how the programs work nor which deficit they claim to remediate.

On the other end of the spectrum, a micromanaging board is one that believes its members have the right or obligation to direct every aspect of the school district, including management procedures and processes. Board member of this type frequently visit school employees and direct or influence them to change their procedures or practice. These school boards spend the majority of their public meetings debating and advising the superintendent and other district personnel on management and operational details. Because a majority of time is spent on the minutia of operational issues, little time is actually spent on creating a vision or monitoring student achievement or district strategic goals.

In terms of the school board member role, a Balanced Governance model instructs and encourages board members to play a constructive part in monitoring and supporting student progress through *informed oversight*. A Balanced Governance approach encourages boards to go beyond only establishing district end-goals or approving management-crafted policy without board input or understanding. It empowers a board to set and monitor high end-goals for student learning, and to understand the means necessary to reach those ends. Balanced Governance equips boards to use detailed knowledge of learning and teaching to better interact with community stakeholders, and craft targeted policy language that intelligently oversees formative progress on adopted processes and programs. The following are a few examples of how a board might apply the Balanced Governance approach in the areas of policy writing and community relations.

Balanced Governance in Policy Writing.   In the area of policy writing, a board practicing at the uninformed delegation end of the governance continuum (see figure I.2) adopts the following policy regarding student achievement in math:

> Math scores will increase by 20% by spring on the State achievement exam.

Notice that this policy follows the "rules" of uninformed delegation by simply setting the numerical outcome standard and remaining uninformed about the processes to achieve the outcome. As a comparison, the board operating at the micromanagement extreme of the governance continuum might adopt a policy as follows:

> Math scores will increase by 20% by spring on the State achievement exam. Board members will spend time in schools to ensure the adopted program is implemented properly. Those teachers not meeting the goal will have reduced pay and be put on a plan of improvement.

Note that in the second example, the school board members are micromanaging by directly influencing methods of implementation of the math improvement. While most micromanaging boards or board members may not construct policies like this, they engage in actions like those depicted in the policy language. The Balanced Governance approach would support the practice of neither uninformed delegation nor micromanagement. Highly effective boards engaged in Balanced Governance might construct a policy that reads:

> Cohort-tracked math test scores on multiple measures (classroom work, class content tests, State exam) showing student growth (classroom assessments and district scores on standardized exams), and disaggregated by socioeconomic status and ethnicity, will be presented quarterly to the school board. The board will use the data to monitor the effectiveness of focused math reform programs, track progress toward district strategic goals, and consider recommendations to retool or replace existing reform programs.

A board creating this example of a Balanced Governance policy is practicing informed oversight. The board members are knowledgeable about which students are experiencing which math issues. Board members understand the component of the math reform that addresses and promises to resolve deficiencies. Board members hold the superintendent accountable to report the progress on the re-form, identify challenges, and make recommendations for improving the reform. Note that Balanced Governance board members, while staying informed about the needs and the remedies, do not engage in suggesting what program should be used or how it should be implemented. Neither does the policy allow board members to influence school personnel directly in the implementation of the program. Finally, Balanced Governance avoids all-or-nothing numerical goals. Board members understand that some students may need more time and special instruction to succeed. As such, if achievement standards are set, they tend to be achievement *growth*, and not absolute one-size-fits-all achievement numbers.

Balanced Governance in Community Relations.   Another area of importance is the board members' role of interacting with the community. The Balanced Governance approach applies to this area as well. For example, a board member practicing at the uninformed delegation side of the governance continuum might communicate to a concerned community member as follows:

> "You don't understand how hard our teachers work."
> "We use research-based best practices to ensure all kids can learn."
> "It is not the school's fault . . . it's broken families."

Note that using this approach, the board member operates as either a benign cheerleader, general critic, or buck-passer. In general, this approach does not lead to community support for the district nor to substantive improvement of district programs. In this case, the public will likely conclude that the board member is uninformed and uninterested in leading real improvement and functioning in a rubber-stamp capacity.

A board member operating at the micromanagement end of the governance continuum might say the following:

> "If our teachers and administrators don't meet the goals, they will eventually not work here anymore."
> "Board members must monitor what is happening in schools because school employees will naturally spin things for their own benefit."
> "I have no problem criticizing failures in board meetings to demonstrate that I am doing my job of ensuring accountability."

In this response, the board member suggests that he or she possesses more power than their office provides and encourages community members to "end-run" the school leadership and bring complaints directly to them. This typically does not result in problems being resolved efficiently and introduces fear among district personnel. The outcome likely is increased conflict, a more highly politicized board, higher forced turnover of superintendents and board members, and lower student achievement.[16]

A Balanced Governance approach would support a response to a community member as follows:

> "Let me describe what we're currently doing to improve our math scores. We measure individual student growth and for any student with slower than expected improvement, all schools use a proven program [name it] adapted to meet individual student needs and local community goals. We monitor the student progress quarterly and show 150% growth for most students. Alternative programs [name them] are being used for the 10% of students not showing growth. For example, [share a specific intervention story]."

This response demonstrates the Balanced Governance approach of informed oversight. The school board member is knowledgeable about the district needs and the programs used to address those needs. Their support or criticism of the district efforts is informed and constructive. Efforts for solutions are expressed as a joint responsibility without placing blame, abdicating oversight responsibility, or promising to micromanage.

Highly effective boards can be identified by their use of a balanced approach to governance and could have come to use a Balanced Governance style—many through an organic, iterative process. Indeed, high achieving boards currently function in a Balanced Governance manner even if they don't use the term. As such, Balanced Governance serves as a descriptor of values, beliefs, and actions that we have found to be highly effective for elected school boards. The chapters that follow provide practical examples of school board training programs, standards, assessments, and recommendations from research, as well as descriptions of highly effective boards. In all cases, these approaches support and exemplify Balanced Governance.

1

Board Leadership That Matters Most

Lessons Learned from the Lighthouse Studies

Mary L. Delagardelle

INTRODUCTION

Until recently, school boards have not typically sought or been encouraged to play an active role in instructional reform efforts leading to improved student achievement. Generally, boards and superintendents feel more comfortable leaving instructional matters solely in the hands of the professional staff. However, the increasing public demand for accountability for student learning places emphasis on the responsibility of the board, as a governing body, to participate more fully in the creation of the vision and direction for student learning. It also requires that the board monitor results of student achievement initiatives, in addition to setting policy and providing resources for improvement efforts.[1]

School boards are charged with approving policy decisions that affect what students learn, how students are taught, how learning is measured, how teachers are supported with professional development, how funds are focused on district priorities, and how effectively the community is engaged around student learning. While by their nature school boards are removed from the day-to-day work of teaching and learning, their policy, personnel, and budgetary decisions control the conditions that support successful teaching and learning throughout the system.

The public cry for improved achievement and accountability in public schools and the traditional lack of board involvement in issues related to student achievement create an urgent need to clearly understand and balance the leadership role of the board as it relates to improving student learning. A better understanding of how board members establish effective district priorities, how the attitudes and beliefs of the board members influence priorities, and which board actions will most likely result in a shared commitment to priorities for student learning is critical for systemic change and student achievement.[2]

The Lighthouse research, funded and supported by the Iowa Association of School Boards, the Iowa School Boards Foundation, and the U.S. Department of Education, was a multiphase, multiyear, and multimethod study to develop understanding about the leadership role of the school board in public education.[3] The series of studies spanning thirteen years asked several important questions, including:

- Are school boards in high achieving districts different from boards in low achieving districts in how they approach their responsibilities?
- What are the specific actions of boards that positively affect district efforts to improve student achievement?
- What are the best practices of board-superintendent team leadership that can be learned by others?

The emerging answers to these questions, resulting from the Lighthouse studies, provide insights into the role of local school boards that matter most for improving student learning.

The Concept of Proximity

In an effort to understand how the Lighthouse study results lead to the improvement of practice embodied in these questions, it is important to introduce the concept of proximity. For many years, researchers have tried to determine the aspects of the school experience that are most likely to make a difference in student learning outcomes. For the sake of this discussion, conditions surrounding teaching and learning are placed on a continuum ranging from those closest to the students and teachers (called *proximal* conditions) and those that are farther away (called *distal* conditions).

As we think about a school system and the conditions most likely to affect student learning, we consider the elements of the school district that most directly influence the student (i.e., that are most proximal). Proximal conditions include the interaction between the student and the teacher around the instructional content, instructional strategies, and the learning environment created in the classroom. It is evident that proximal conditions are likely to have the most influence on improving student learning. Governance processes, including school board policy decisions, are much farther away (distal) from the student. However, studies now are finding that distal conditions can also have a significant effect on student learning when they directly affect proximal conditions, that is, when they influence the conditions of practice within the district or affect the learning environment within the schools and classrooms.

Although the board-superintendent team operate "at a distance" from the learner, their goal must always be to strengthen districtwide conditions of practice that affect the learning environment within the schools and classrooms. The Lighthouse studies demonstrate that board-superintendent teams are not too far removed from the work of teaching and learning to have an influence on student learning. Indeed, the importance of recognizing the influence of distal as well as proximal conditions leads to a realistic consideration of the importance of school board decisions and actions and how they can be more effective. Figure 1.1 illustrates the linkages showing the potential influence of the school board on student learning.

While only 35 percent of school board members are professional educators,[4] the Lighthouse research provides convincing evidence that board members can have significant influence on teaching and learning, curriculum and instruction, and the learning environment. A Balanced Governance approach, exemplified by the Lighthouse governance process, does not support the notion that board members need to become educational experts. Indeed, recent findings by Shober and Hartney[5] confirm that school boards composed of a majority of educators are not linked to improved student achievement. The Lighthouse studies do suggest that school board members need to develop sufficient understanding, knowledge, and beliefs in order to create the conditions within the system that will ensure that professional educators can grow in their educational expertise and generate productive change. School board members can enhance their leadership role in

Figure 1.1 Important linkages

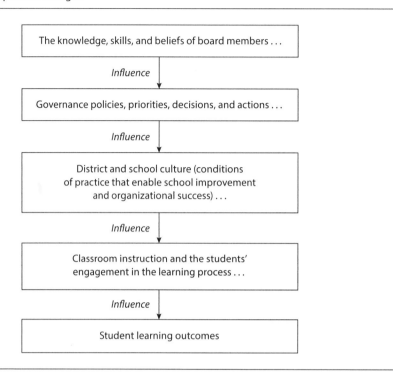

the school renewal process without digressing into micromanaging the system. This chapter shares key findings from the Lighthouse research that shed light on important board behaviors, within a balanced approach to governance, that positively affect district efforts to improve student learning.

BOARD-SUPERINTENDENT TEAM LEADERSHIP

Key Board Actions That Generate Conditions for Productive Change

The conditions within a school district that have been shown to enable productive change in student learning are relatively consistent across studies even though the labels to describe them may be slightly different. Consistently high achieving districts, or districts that have significantly improved achievement, often attribute their success to the following:

- Clear goals and measurable targets for improving student learning
- Extensive use of data to inform and monitor improvement efforts
- An infrastructure within the school and district that supports collaboration, innovation, and research
- Support for ongoing professional learning that is focused on collaborative inquiry into teaching and learning
- High levels of engagement with parents and the community
- Strong leadership at all levels of the system to guide and protect the work

These conditions of practice are well researched, and there appears to be agreement about the importance of these conditions for producing positive change in student learning outcomes. However, the large-scale presence of these conditions in districts and schools is still lacking. The Lighthouse research supports the possibility that the missing piece in many efforts to improve achievement may be a lack of focus by the leadership at the school board and superintendent level. Specifically, the study results point to the negative effects of a lack of school board and superintendent focus on generating the conditions for student improvement listed above. The conditions described above are system conditions and cannot be adequately managed at a building level without the support of the entire system. Efforts to improve achievement that assume the building is the unit of change and the principal is the most important change leader are not wrong, they just neglect to include the system-level leadership necessary to ensure that the principal's work at the building level can generate the desired results and be sustained over time.

The Lighthouse studies identified seven areas of board action and the specific knowledge, skills, and beliefs necessary for effective performance in each of those areas (see table 1.1). When boards worked together to build their knowledge and take specific actions, grounded in elevating beliefs about what was possible to accomplish, the culture of the schools improved, the beliefs of the adults became more elevating, and the achievement of students improved.[6]

Table 1.1 Key actions of the board using the Lighthouse approach: An example of a Balanced Governance model

Key areas of board action	Knowledge, skills, and beliefs necessary for positive impact
Developing awareness of the student learning needs, and building commitment to systemically address the needs • Clarifying the current status of student learning and the student learning needs • Increasing a sense of urgency • Using data to focus efforts on the area of greatest learning need • Improving the interactions between the teacher and the student around content (instruction) as the key means to improve learning • Expecting more • Believing it's possible	**Know** • Understand what's at stake if nothing changes (in relation to student learning) • Understand that improving teaching is the most important factor for improving student learning • Understand the importance of improving teaching in the content area of greatest student learning need • Confront their beliefs about what is possible to expect in terms of student learning; understand what is possible to expect (learn from schools that have beat the odds) • Understand the current status of student learning in their district, based on analysis of data • Understand the learning gaps that exist among subgroups of students and how they could be addressed • Understand that boards make a difference (board leadership is critical for improving learning for all students) **Do** • Communicate the urgency for improving student learning • Consistently communicate high expectations • Use data and research to identify the highest priorities for change, define a clear and narrow focus for improvement, and identify specific short-term targets for monitoring progress • Communicate the focus for improvement and model adherence to the focus through board actions and conversations **Believe** • The current level of student achievement is not what we can expect—we can expect much more • How well students learn in school depends primarily upon what the adults in the school do • Improving the quality of teaching is the most important strategy for improving student learning • Virtually all children can meet grade-level expectations • We have become complacent about the achievement of our students

Key areas of board action	Knowledge, skills, and beliefs necessary for positive impact
Applying pressure for accountability • Using data extensively • Setting high expectations for improvement • Defining acceptable evidence • Monitoring progress constantly	**Know** • Understand the important role of pressure and support (accountability and reciprocal responsibility) • Understand key data analysis concepts • Understand the importance of monitoring both implementation and impact • Understand the school culture necessary for improving student learning and key indicators of that culture • Understand the current status of achievement in the district and what needs to change • Understand what are reasonable targets for improvement given the current achievement status **Do** • Set improvement goals and targets that appropriately "stretch" the district improvement efforts • Identify the indicators the board will accept as evidence of progress toward the goal and/or targets • Regularly monitor progress toward specific annual targets • Ensure that conditions necessary for continuous improvement are present in the culture of the school and regularly monitor evidence of progress toward a learning culture for adults and students • Expect and support corrective action when progress is not evident (in the culture, in the implementation of improvement efforts, and in the impact on student learning) • Discuss the implications of data reports and references data in decision making and problem solving • Support decisions with good data and information (internal and external—cost and impact) **Believe** • Frequent monitoring of student learning is critical to improving teaching and learning • Both formative and summative assessments of student learning are critical for monitoring progress

continued

Table 1.1 *continued*

Key areas of board action	Knowledge, skills, and beliefs necessary for positive impact
Demonstrating commitment	**Know**
• Creating board learning time	• The role of the board for improving achievement
• Spending time learning together as a board team	• The public/governing role of the board in relation to democratic principles
• Modeling a willingness to learn and innovate	• Key principles of balanced governance
• Focusing board conversations around what matters most—student learning	**Do**
	• Focus board meetings on the improvement area
• Staying the course	• Use an agreed-upon framework for conversations among board members and with the staff that helps maintain the focus for the conversations/discussions
• Demonstrating commitment to the focus area for improvement through board actions and decisions (resource allocation, time provision, calendar, negotiations, etc.)	• Commit extra board time for work sessions to focus on the area the district is trying to improve and board learning in relation to the focus area
	• Demonstrate commitment through
	– Negotiations
	– Calendar development
	– Budget setting
	– Policy development and approval
	– Superintendent selection
	– Superintendent evaluation
	• Evaluate the performance of the board based on the collective effort to monitor, support, and ensure that the district improvement goals are met
	Believe
	• In order for student learning to improve, schools must be organized and structured differently
	• Schools cannot continue to do what they have always done and expect to get different results
	• Doing more of what we are currently doing will not result in significantly improved learning

Key areas of board action	Knowledge, skills, and beliefs necessary for positive impact
Providing support for ongoing professional learning • Setting clear expectations (outcomes and process) • Creating time • Providing financial support • Celebrating success	**Know** • Standards for professional learning (what it takes to change practice at the classroom level in ways that will have a positive impact on student learning) • The board's role in relation to selecting improvement initiatives and providing the system of professional learning that is necessary to support them • The criteria to consider when approving and supporting initiatives to improve achievement • The implications of fully implementing potential initiatives to improve achievement (includes general understanding of what it will take for full implementation) **Do** • Analyze the current professional learning system in relation to what it takes to change practice • Consider initiatives to improve achievement from a framework of key criteria • Analyze the cost effectiveness of current and potential initiatives to improve achievement • Set clear/measurable expectations for the outcomes of professional learning (student learning improves as the primary outcome) • Allocate resources to ensure that a district infrastructure exists to support quality professional learning • Allocate resources to ensure the success of approved initiatives to improve achievement • Monitor progress/success of professional learning in relation to the implementation of initiatives and the established outcomes **Believe** • In order to change outcomes for students, we must continuously invest in building the capacity of the educators • School districts must focus major attention on building cultures of collaborative inquiry to continuously build the capacity of the educators • Collaboration among adults is necessary for substantially improving student learning • Student achievement barriers, such as poverty and lack of family support, can be overcome by the most effective instructional practices

continued

Table 1.1 *continued*

Key areas of board action	Knowledge, skills, and beliefs necessary for positive impact
Supporting and connecting with districtwide leadership • Building the capacity of the board/superintendent team to provide districtwide leadership for improving student learning • Establishing a district leadership team • Connecting regularly with the district leadership team • Establishing a willingness and readiness to lead and let others lead from their respective roles	**Know** • The leadership role of the board • The importance of distributed leadership • The difference between leadership and management • The instructional leadership role of school administrators • The characteristics of the leadership needed for improving student achievement • The importance of a narrow focus for improvement • A framework for receiving and responding to reports from staff regarding student learning during board meetings and work sessions **Do** • Establish clarity, systemwide, about the most important focus for improving student learning • Communicate consistently about the focus for improvement, the specific expectations/targets, and what the district is doing to improve achievement • Protect the work from fragmentation and distraction • Stay the course • Monitor progress regularly and ensure that corrective action is taken and supported when needed **Believe** • Leadership is either everywhere or it is nowhere • Leadership for improving teaching and learning is critical to school district success

Key areas of board action	Knowledge, skills, and beliefs necessary for positive impact
Participating in a deliberative policy development process	**Know** • The difference between discussion and deliberation • The importance of whole-board deliberation throughout the policy development process (for policies directly impacting teaching and learning) • The role of policy for guiding and sustaining district work **Do** • Study background information related to the policy area • Identify greatest hopes • Prioritize expectations • Determine measures of progress/success for each expectation • Identify support needs for each expectation • Finalize priority expectations based on what can be monitored and supported • Regularly monitor policy implementation **Believe** • Local school governance is critical for ensuring the success of all students • Local school boards can positively impact teaching and learning • The actions and beliefs of board members is critical to district success

continued

Table 1.1 *continued*

Key areas of board action	Knowledge, skills, and beliefs necessary for positive impact

Connecting with the community and building the public will to improve achievement	**Know**
	• The importance of the school connecting with the community and the community connecting with the school
	• The different levels of community connection
	  – Informed
	  – Input
	  – Involvement
	  – Engagement
	• What must change, and why, in order to establish a productive school/community relationship
	• Key talking points for
	  – what must change in terms of learning and the learning environment
	  – the compelling reasons for making the change
	  – what the community should expect to see in terms of progress
	  – how the community can help
	
	Do
	• Value the important role of the community in helping the district meet its goals
	• Value the role of the school within the larger community (other child-serving organizations) and understand the specific contribution of each organization
	• Consistently communicate the reason for change and the vision for the future
	• Consistently communicate what the district is trying to improve, specific expectations, what the district is doing to reach the expectations, and how the community can help
	
	Believe
	• The community must be a partner with the school district in order for the school to improve learning for all students

KEY BOARD ACTIONS THAT PROMOTE STUDENT IMPROVEMENT

Nested in the board actions described in table 1.1 are three areas that were consistent starting points for boards wanting to strengthen their leadership and their influence on district efforts to improve student learning. Before anything else, boards need to be willing to create urgency for improving achievement within their district and their community, collectively commit to high expectations, and understand the role of pressure and support in relation to governance and continuous improvement.

Creating Urgency

In order to create urgency for improving achievement, board members in the Lighthouse districts had to first be clear about the current status of achievement in their districts. This was much more than just looking at the data and hearing reports about the status of achievement as most boards do already.[7] They rolled up their sleeves and worked with other district leaders to deeply study the data, complete reflection protocols related to the data study, engage in deep discussions about what the data were telling them and what the data were *not* telling them, generate additional questions they would like to be able to answer, and talk with their staff about the implications and needs that surfaced from the data study.

However, this deeper data study about the current status of student achievement was not enough to create a shared sense of urgency. Board members also had to believe that more was possible to expect of student performance. Many district leaders indicate they are doing about as well as can be expected given the backgrounds of the students they serve.[8] These leaders appear to be communicating an underlying belief that factors outside the school are *determiners* of student success rather than *predictors* of student success. It was not until board members studied outstanding student performance outcomes from districts with students that are hardest to teach, and became convinced that more is possible in their district as well, that a sense of urgency began to surface.

After being confronted with the data about their current status and the data from other places showing what is possible to accomplish, board members had to make it personal in terms of the students and families they served. This included the need for the school board to wrestle with deepening their understanding of what is at stake for students if nothing changes, and to confront their own willingness to do whatever it takes to ensure excellence for all students. These changes in belief were necessary before school boards were willing to talk about the urgent need to improve achievement with their staff and their community. Board members are much more practiced at being "cheerleaders" for their schools and sharing pride in their school and district than they are at sharing what needs to improve, what they are doing to improve it, and why that is so important. In the Lighthouse training, school board members learn to create stories that both present the data and tug at the heartstrings to be able to communicate effectively what must improve as well as why people should be proud of their system. Interestingly, when done well and communicated without blame or shame, the staff and community seem to embrace the honest assessment of the needs and are more willing to engage in the hard work of change.

As the sense of urgency and the resulting increase in focus and action emerged, so did an increased passion for excellence. As one board member said, "We were very satisfied being good, but now we want to be great!" As board members and staff learned to work together more constructively, failure was no longer an option for any child. They were on a journey to excellence and a relentless pursuit of the best practices that would help them get there.

Commitment to High Expectations

School boards in the successful Lighthouse districts made an obvious commitment to high expectations for improving student learning. They had a strong, shared belief that improved outcomes were possible to expect and that the district had the capacity to create positive change for all students. They did not make excuses for student learning even though their districts were experiencing the same challenges and changing demographics as other districts. They knew that the central core of what schooling is all about—the interaction between the student and the teacher around content—had to be the focus of the district's work, and that everything else was peripheral to the core. They spent time together establishing improvement goals and targets, learning about the district's efforts to improve achievement, and ensuring that they could all consistently communicate the student learning needs the district was trying to improve. In addition, board members became adept at communicating what the district was doing to improve student achievement, why they believed they would get the results they wanted, and how they were monitoring progress.

Goal setting in the Lighthouse districts became an interactive process between the board-superintendent team and the districtwide leadership team. Typically, district administration and staff establish the goals for improvement and the board approves them.[9] However, the boards in the Lighthouse districts soon realized that without more involvement in the establishment of the goals, they did not have the sense of ownership and commitment that was necessary to make the difficult decisions and provide necessary support. The boards realized that they had fallen into a pattern of approving the goals, hearing annual reports about progress, and then congratulating the district for all the hard work in failing to reach the goals. To break this cycle, the following framework (see table 1.2), defining various components of a districtwide school improvement goal, was useful for helping school boards become meaningful participants in the goal setting and monitoring process without micromanaging the process or engaging in the process in isolation of their district administrators and staff.

Pressure and Support

Elmore,[10] in his landmark piece on school leadership, discusses the concept of reciprocity of accountability. Essentially, he makes the case that anyone in a position of leadership with the authority to hold someone accountable for accomplishing something, has a reciprocal responsibility to make sure they have everything they need to accomplish it. In the context of the Lighthouse work, boards realized they have the authority to hold the superintendent responsible for accomplishing the improvement goals of the district and, therefore, have the reciprocal responsibility to make sure that the superintendent has everything he or she needs to accomplish them. Boards also realized that the best measure of their effectiveness was the degree to which they created the conditions, provided the support, and enabled the superintendent to do what they had asked of him or her. This created a need for a different type of relationship between the board and the superintendent. In order to provide this type of reciprocal support, the board-superintendent team

Table 1.2 Components of districtwide improvement goals

Component	Characteristics	Example(s)	Sample board questions
Districtwide improvement goal	Clear statement about what we are trying to collectively improve. • Focused on student learning in a content area • Related to the greatest student learning need at this time • Short term • Includes each of the components described below	Increase the number of students demonstrating proficiency in reading comprehension by 10% while maintaining or increasing the number of students performing above grade level as indicated by multiple measures of reading comprehension by May, 20XX. (Measures include but are not limited to: Series assessments, Jamestown Reader, BRI, MAP tests, Iowa Tests)	See questions related to each component of the goal statement.
Content area of greatest student learning need	The content area where data indicate the most students are non-proficient. • Multiple data sources confirm the need	• Increase the number of students demonstrating proficiency in reading. • Increase the number of students demonstrating proficiency in mathematics.	• What must we improve right now? What area must we put our collective energy into improving (evidence of need across levels)? • As we study our students' achievement data, which content area appears to be our lowest area across the most levels? Are we confident that is our area of greatest need? Do we have multiple sources of evidence that this is our greatest need?
Narrow focus for improvement	A specific strand within the broad content area that focuses improvement efforts. • Broad enough that all levels can contribute • Narrow enough so the efforts aren't fragmented or disjointed • Based on greatest student learning need	• Increase the number of students demonstrating proficiency in reading comprehension. • Increase the number of students demonstrating proficiency in complex mathematical problem solving.	• More specifically, what are we trying to improve? • What strand within the content area needs the most attention? How do we know? • Is there clear evidence of need in relation to this strand? • Is this an area that spans all grade levels? Are the needs similar at different levels across the system? • How will different levels be able to contribute to improvement in this strand? Will the focus need to be different at different levels?

Component	Characteristics	Example(s)	Sample board questions
Specific measurable targets for improvement	Specific indicators of progress so it is clear when we are making progress toward the goal and when the goal has been reached. • Focused on results • Should include measures that allow for ongoing monitoring of progress (will need to identify measures/types of assessments and define a schedule for monitoring progress) • Describes sufficient stretch—ambitious but realistic improvement	• Increase the number of students proficient in reading comprehension by 10% as evidenced by performance on districtwide measures of reading comprehension such as BRI, MAP, Jamestown Reader, and Iowa Tests (using the measure of grade level proficiency defined by each assessment). • *May also want to include how often this will be monitored:* Progress will be reviewed by staff during their study teams each week and reviewed by the board at least once each quarter.	• What level of improvement do we want to see? What's the performance we hope to see in our data? • Is the improvement target ambitious enough to produce worthwhile change in student performance? • Is the improvement target realistic—with collective effort is it reasonable to assume we could succeed? • What districtwide measures are available for us to monitor progress? How frequently do they allow us to monitor progress? Do we have enough regular/ongoing assessments across levels that are valid and reliable to provide us with good information on a regular basis? • Will we need different indicators of progress for different levels? • What do we know about student growth (over time) in this area as well as their current level of attainment? • Are there subgroups of students (who perform less well in this area) that we need to be monitoring while we monitor overall districtwide progress?
Timeline for improvement	• Defines the deadline for completion	• 10% increase by May, 2011	• How soon do we hope to see change in performance? • Is the timeline reasonable in relation to the target? How do we know? • What will it take? Are we willing to provide the necessary support to ensure success? • Are we clear about the actions it will take to meet the goal? Can they be taken effectively within this time frame?

needed to be convinced of the importance and reasonableness of the improvement goals. In addition, they needed to trust each other in ways they had not previously pursued, communicate in ways that had not previously been necessary, and be willing to let each other provide strong leadership from their respective roles. This concept of reciprocity of accountability helped the boards understand a key role of the board for providing "pressure and support." Pressure comes from the clear expectations laid out in the improvement goals and targets for the district and the unwavering expectation from the board that the district will be successful in accomplishing those goals. Support comes from the willingness of the board to make sure the superintendent has everything needed to accomplish the goals. Pressure and support as an ongoing interaction includes collaboratively setting goals, determining what it will take to accomplish the goals, negotiating the expectations based on the support needed, providing the support, monitoring progress, and adjusting actions to ensure success. This act of finding the right balance of both pressure and support becomes a significant role of the board relating to improving student achievement.

SUMMARY

A great deal is already known about what it takes to improve the achievement of all students in classrooms and schools. Numerous studies and books have been written describing the characteristics of more effective learning environments. Numerous examples of schools that beat the odds and produce high levels of learning for all students exist. However, less is known about what it takes to lead an entire district to high levels of learning and sustain a culture focused on excellence and equity. Until recently, school boards have been excluded from the school reform literature and excluded from consideration as a unit of change or a key lever in the change process. The Lighthouse studies and the tools, processes, and studies described in this book open the door to understanding how to help local school governance play a role that positively impacts the learning of students in their schools. Each exemplar of the Balanced Governance approach encourages school board members to act not as managers of the school but as governors of the system and important leaders of systemic change in concert with their administrators, teachers, and community.

2

Transforming Beliefs into Action

Board and Superintendent Teams Working Together

Tom Shelton

The United States practices a decentralized system of schooling in which the states historically assign responsibility for school governance to locally elected school boards. In practice, school boards charge a local superintendent with the management of local schools; however, over the past three decades boards have begun to take a much more active role in the management, operations, and personnel of their schools. Many believe this change has been driven by the increasing demands placed on America's local school boards to raise students' academic achievement.[1] Unfortunately, there has been limited research into what role a school board can play in responding to these demands.[2]

THE PURPOSE OF SCHOOL BOARDS

In the United States, school boards were created to ensure local governance of a free public education. Some 96 percent of American school boards are locally elected, making that model the most prevalent form of governance to date.[3] Elected boards are intended to provide each community with a representative voice in how local schools educate their children.

While differing views regarding the primary purpose of school boards are common,[4] many believe a board's focus should be on supporting the improvement of teaching and learning with a view to establishing coherent, attainable outcomes that reflect the community vision for education.

Although research on school board effectiveness is limited, Land described the belief that school boards were critical to supporting students' academic success and that the boards' focus on instructional improvement was gaining momentum.[5] However, she noted that few studies dealt directly with this subject and stressed the importance of the need for more research on how boards may influence student achievement trends in their district.

In studies of districts in several states, Goodman[6] found that districts with quality governance tended to have greater student achievement as measured by dropout rates, the percentage of students going to college, and aptitude test scores. The Iowa Association of School Boards (IASB) conducted a series of rigorous school board effects studies from 2001 to 2014, known as the Lighthouse study,[7] which identified five roles of a board-superintendent team that is focused on student achievement, and provided detailed prescriptions as to how to fulfill these roles. Briefly, the five are: set clear expectations, create conditions for success (such as supporting quality professional development), hold the system accountable, build collective will, and learn together as a team.

Delagardelle[8] observed that a commonly held assumption that school boards should avoid matters dealing with teaching and learning might have drawn school boards away from the very behaviors that are likely to have the greatest impact on student achievement.

The Superintendent's Role

Research on superintendents and their effects on improving student performance is much more common than studies on school board influence. For example, one study[9] focused on the particular activities undertaken by central office administrators linked to improved student achievement, including an established instructional and curricular focus, consistency and coordination of instructional activities, strong instructional leadership from the superintendent, and an emphasis on monitoring instruction and curriculum.

Another study[10] identified five district-level leadership responsibilities having positive correlations with student academic achievement. They recommended establishing nonnegotiable district goals for student achievement and effective instruction as a necessary condition for improving student achievement. These goals should be monitored and used as the basis for immediate corrective action to move districts toward the ideal of high-reliability organizations. Also, the nonnegotiable goals for achievement and instruction should be established through collaborative goal-setting that involves key stakeholders.

Relationships Between School Boards and Superintendents

Surprisingly little research is available on school board–superintendent relationships, and much of what has been done does not focus on the effects of that relationship on student achievement. However, one study[11] found that a primary characteristic of an effective school board in districts with high student achievement is a good working relationship between the board and the superintendent. Some researchers[12] concluded that cooperation and trust among board members and between the board and superintendent are necessary steps toward improving student performance. Other findings conclude that boards and superintendents need to collaborate in a shared role in school district governance if they hope to support increased student achievement.[13]

A study of rapidly improving districts[14] identified the leadership of school boards, along with superintendents, as key factors supporting increased student achievement. Each of the districts the authors studied employed superintendents who developed and nurtured widely shared beliefs about learning, including high expectations, and provided a focus on monitoring student achievement results.

Studies highlight the importance of teamwork between the school board and superintendent. They call for ongoing team-building education and development for the school board and superintendent to achieve high-quality, collaborative governance that effectively improves student achievement.

The study reported in this chapter[15] compared shared school board and superintendent beliefs with improved student achievement. This study was conducted in Kentucky and included 75 percent of the superintendents and 28 percent of the school board members in the state. Both the superintendent and at least one board member completed the survey in 64 percent of the Kentucky districts.

Board-Superintendent Effects on Student Achievement

The survey used in the Kentucky study (see figure 2.1) was slightly modified from the one used in the Lighthouse study.[16] The survey asked board members to rate their perceived *value* of a series of board activities as well as the amount of *time* their board spent on those activities. In addition, superintendents and school board members were asked to describe selected attributes of their board-superintendent relationship linked to highly effective teams that support and promote improved student performance. As such, the survey and its elements could easily be used as an evaluation tool for board performance.

This study found three factors that affected student achievement gains (eighth-grade math) on the Kentucky Commonwealth Accountability Testing System (CATS), namely: time spent by the school board on student achievement monitoring and discussion, the perceived importance of board members engaging in student achievement monitoring and discussion, and the presence of positive and productive superintendent-board relationships.

The Impact of Values and Beliefs on Student Achievement

The results of this study indicate that the most important role of a school board after the selection of a superintendent is to create an environment in which the superintendent can focus his or her time on student achievement. The findings support the need for school boards to focus *with* their superintendents on student achievement, so that superintendents can maintain an academic focus.

Superintendents and school board members in this study were asked a series of questions regarding their perceived effects on student achievement. For example, one question asked what, if any, impact does the working relationship (i.e. understanding and respect of roles) between school board members and superintendents have on district-level student achievement.

The study found that board members and superintendents alike clearly believed they could affect student achievement. Each group believed the relationship between the two was a key to growth in student achievement. However, the superintendents believed that board members typically preferred to spend their time on matters other than student achievement, such as business issues or athletics.

Board members and superintendents indicated they believed that a higher education level of board members and greater years of service by either the board or

Figure 2.1   Survey of school board behaviors linked to high performing schools

INSTRUCTIONS: The items shown below describe topics relating to student achievement and to the right of each item is a 5-point scale to measure the amount of time spent on each topic by your board/superintendent team that ranges from a low of 1 (**Not Much or Negligible Time**) to a high of 5 (**Significant Time**). Please circle the *one* number for each scale that best reflects your opinion regarding your current level of time spent on the topic.

Please indicate the amount of time your board currently spends on the following topics:

1. Discussing improvement in student learning.	1	2	3	4	5
2. Ensuring time exists for staff to work together to improve student learning.	1	2	3	4	5
3. Developing and expressing a belief that the staff can significantly affect student learning.	1	2	3	4	5
4. Establishing criteria to guide the staff in choosing initiatives to improve student learning.	1	2	3	4	5
5. Evaluating the effectiveness of professional development for improving student learning.	1	2	3	4	5
6. Monitoring progress of student learning in relation to improvement goals.	1	2	3	4	5
7. Influencing a community-wide belief that all students can and should be expected to learn the basic skills necessary to succeed in their current grade level.	1	2	3	4	5
8. Mobilizing the community to support the goals for improving student learning.	1	2	3	4	5
9. Ensuring there is strong leadership for improving instruction in ways that result in improved student learning.	1	2	3	4	5
10. Establishing and communicating a singular focus for improving student learning (for example: a primary focus on improving reading comprehension).	1	2	3	4	5
11. Adopting and monitoring long-range and annual improvement goals to improve student learning.	1	2	3	4	5
12. Adopting and monitoring plans for improving student learning.	1	2	3	4	5
13. Adopting and monitoring procedures for regularly informing the community about student learning progress.	1	2	3	4	5
14. Discussing/reviewing legal mandates and rules related to improving student learning.	1	2	3	4	5
15. Ensuring that there is open and honest dialogue and an attitude of mutual trust and respect between board members and the superintendent.	1	2	3	4	5
16. Ensuring that the daily executive responsibility of the superintendent is respected by the board and the governance responsibility of the board is respected by the superintendent.	1	2	3	4	5

Figure 2.1   *continued*

INSTRUCTIONS: The items shown below describe various topics relating to student achievement and to the right of each item is a 5-point scale to measure your perception of the importance of each topic that ranges from a low of 1 (**Not Very Important**) to a high of 5 (**Very Important**). Please circle the *one* number for each scale that best reflects your opinion regarding the importance of the following task.

Please indicate your perception of the importance your board places on the following topics:

1. Discussing improvement in student learning.	1	2	3	4	5
2. Ensuring time exists for staff to work together to improve student learning.	1	2	3	4	5
3. Developing and expressing a belief that the staff can significantly affect student learning.	1	2	3	4	5
4. Establishing criteria to guide the staff in choosing initiatives to improve student learning.	1	2	3	4	5
5. Evaluating the effectiveness of professional development for improving student learning.	1	2	3	4	5
6. Monitoring progress of student learning in relation to improvement goals.	1	2	3	4	5
7. Influencing a community-wide belief that all students can and should be expected to learn the basic skills necessary to succeed in their current grade level.	1	2	3	4	5
8. Mobilizing the community to support the goals for improving student learning.	1	2	3	4	5
9. Ensuring there is strong leadership for improving instruction in ways that result in improved student learning.	1	2	3	4	5
10. Establishing and communicating a singular focus for improving student learning (for example: a primary focus on improving reading comprehension).	1	2	3	4	5
11. Adopting and monitoring long-range and annual improvement goals to improve student learning.	1	2	3	4	5
12. Adopting and monitoring plans for improving student learning.	1	2	3	4	5
13. Adopting and monitoring procedures for regularly informing the community about student learning progress.	1	2	3	4	5
14. Discussing/reviewing legal mandates and rules related to improving student learning.	1	2	3	4	5
15. Ensuring that there is open and honest dialogue and an attitude of mutual trust and respect between board members and the superintendent.	1	2	3	4	5
16. Ensuring that the daily executive responsibility of the superintendent is respected by the board and the governance responsibility of the board is respected by the superintendent.	1	2	3	4	5

superintendent correspond with greater student achievement. Both groups believed that the time and importance placed on the values and beliefs they held about student achievement would be reflected in the math achievement scores. However, superintendents felt it was their responsibility to focus the board on student achievement and to clearly communicate the importance of this emphasis. Improvement of student learning occurs first and foremost in the classroom, but findings from this study indicate important roles for school boards and superintendents as well.

1. Boards and superintendents independently agreed on the importance of three factors: valuing achievement outcomes, allocating time to those outcomes, and the importance of positive board-superintendent relationships. Both groups felt that a team approach was most likely to be successful.

2. A board with, on average, more formal education was more likely to relate to higher academic achievement. This was shown quantitatively and affirmed by board member focus groups.

3. The best single measure of student achievement gain, after accounting for socioeconomic status, was the extent to which the superintendent reported spending more time focused on academics. Both superintendents and board members were in agreement on this point. This focus could be gained by a superintendent working together with the board, or independently of the board, as long as the board did not foster a disruptive climate.

4. General superintendent turnover was associated with a one-year drop in mathematics achievement, but with a long-term greater improvement in the same measure. This points to the importance of distinguishing between destabilizing superintendent turnover (e.g., pressured turnover) and general turnover (e.g., moving to a larger district). This supports Alsbury's findings that apolitical superintendent turnover resulted in only a short-term achievement drop, while disruptive, political, or destabilizing superintendent turnover resulted in long-term achievement decline.[17]

Guidelines for School Board Practice

This research produced a list of guidelines likely to improve the practice of boards and superintendents. These include:

1. Superintendents need to have a laser focus on student achievement and devote a large portion of their time to enhancing it.
2. School boards need to create environments that have administrative leadership focused on improving student achievement.
3. Board members and superintendents are well advised to focus some shared professional development on team building for student achievement. Clarity of roles and the reduction of conflict increase the time that can be spent on student achievement.
4. Hiring and evaluation of a new superintendent should focus on the leader's time and effectiveness with regard to student achievement results.
5. Communities, advocacy groups, and school board associations could use data from this study to promote interest among quality candidates.

CONCLUSION

Earlier in this chapter, prior research suggesting that community and student demographics relate to student achievement. Figure 2.2 reflects a revised school board–superintendent effects model on student achievement based on the find-

Figure 2.2 Revised theoretical school board and superintendent effects model

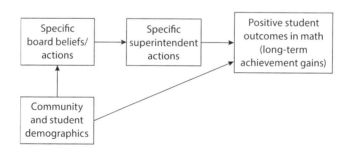

- Student/community demographics are important in understanding the beginning level of mean achievement among students, but not the rate of upward growth from a baseline.
- Specific superintendent actions (time spent) on student achievement will cause gains in student achievement over time.
- A specific set of beliefs and actions held by the school board can, over the long term, affect the superintendent's time spent on student achievement, thus causing gains over time.

ings of this study, indicating that a board-superintendent relationship may affect student achievement.

We do not yet know if there is a different effect on student achievement when comparing a board that creates an environment of expectations of growth and holds the superintendent accountable with a board that simply stays out of the way of an achievement-focused superintendent. It is clear that a superintendent who focuses on student achievement can have a significant impact. However, it is critical that the board support this focus and actions strengthening the board-superintendent team and creating the expectation of student success.

Previous studies reflected a belief that certain values, beliefs, and actions of a school board would directly affect the growth in student achievement.[18] The Kentucky study, in contrast, measured the effects of a superintendent's values, beliefs, and actions on such achievement. The sum of the values, beliefs, and actions of both parties were thought to be greater than the impact of either by itself. The results indicated that if a board does not create the appropriate environment for the superintendent—either by setting and supporting expectations of student achievement or by not interfering in a superintendent's actions focused on this outcome—then student achievement will not improve at a high rate. The model in figure 2.2 better reflects the effect of school board–superintendent teams on improving student achievement.

Some have suggested that the most important role of the board is the selection of the superintendent. If the board expects growth in student achievement, the results of this study support this conclusion only when coupled with a healthy relationship between the superintendent and the school board. When the results from this study are analyzed they clearly indicate that both board members and superintendents must function as a team to be effective—that is, the relationship must remain balanced. In other words, this study does not support governance models that promote dominance from either the superintendent (as when the board simply delegates and defers to him or her) or the board (as with a micromanaging board). The model in figure 2.2 reflects a belief that the sum of the two working as a team has a greater impact than either individually.

The study presented in this chapter indicates that the superintendent is most influential in the quality of the board-superintendent relationship. In addition, the study indicates that student achievement data influences the superintendent's decision-making style and influences, positively or negatively, how they interact with the board.

Until recently, school boards and superintendents were only rarely considered as a potential unit of change or a key lever in the change process. This study suggests new mechanisms for understanding how to help board-superintendent teams play a role that positively affects the learning of students in their schools.

3

School Boards in Their Environment

Balancing Brokerage and Closure

Argun Saatcioglu

There are competing views on the value of school boards for educational governance and reform. Some view boards as obsolete entities that deter progress and innovation,[1] while others emphasize the critical role of boards as agents of public voice. Traditionally, school boards represent local community preferences for the education of their children, critical for the legitimacy of public education and for effective policy implementation and outcomes.[2] Much of this debate is "ideological," given the absence of strong evidence for views advocated by either side. Solid research into the effects of school boards on key outcomes such as student achievement and the efficient use of resources has been growing.[3] However, current research has not yet provided enough clear evidence on the effectiveness of schools boards. Neither has it adequately supported practical guidelines on how to make school boards function effectively to improve educational and other critical outcomes. This is an important gap, particularly in an era when the quality and promise of educational practices and policies are increasingly questioned unless they are "evidenced-based."

Previous work by Saatcioglu and Sargut develops and tests a model of school board effectiveness in light of a concept known as social capital.[4] A formal task group improves its social capital when members develop cohesive relationships with one another along with constructive relationships with external actors and institutions in the policy environment that can provide the group with important information, support, and ideas for innovation. This chapter addresses practical ways to cultivate social capital in school boards through measuring and balancing internal working relationships (closure) and external ties (brokerage). The assessment of closure and brokerage on school boards represents a way to help boards move toward a Balanced Governance approach. It involves using diagnostic tools to evaluate school board closure and brokerage and providing recommendations for balancing these important elements and increasing social capital while improving student achievement.

SCHOOL BOARD SOCIAL CAPITAL

At the most basic level, school boards are influenced by two realities: internal relations among board members and external relations with other stakeholders in the community. These are critical elements when measuring social capital in organizations: how well do members work with one another, and what outside connections do they have? Both these relationships are important for school board effectiveness. Not only do members need to work together in a productive and collegial fashion, they also benefit from a wide variety of connections to external entities that influence their work, such as legislators, civic groups, parents, universities, news media, business leaders, philanthropists, and leaders and administrators in other districts. These external influences can be a source of information, resources, innovative ideas, and legitimacy for the board and district.

Existing research on school boards supports the importance of internal and external relationships. However, the research remains incomplete because past studies typically address internal and external relationships as separate entities. Social capital theory provides a unifying framework, combining the influence of internal and external school board relationships to form a larger picture. Of particular importance is Ronald Burt's work in which he defines internal board relationship as *closure* and external board relationship as *brokerage*.[5] His model compares the importance of these two influences and predicts that performance in groups such as organizational boards is highest when both closure and brokerage are at high levels.

This chapter reviews insights from school board research in this area and discusses how the closure/brokerage model provides important implications for practice.

Understanding Closure and Brokerage

Closure refers to the quality of member relations within the group. It involves trust, cooperation, and mutual respect. Limited closure leads to individuals acting for their own interests rather than the good of the entire organization[6]—a pattern that is all too common in dysfunctional boards.[7] Such boards tend to experience ongoing power struggles,[8] causing districts to lose significant resources, miss opportunities, and lose legitimacy within their communities.[9] In addition, board membership may be viewed as a means to advance one's own career[10] and/or a vehicle to address the needs of only specific constituents.[11] Higher levels of closure reduce the risk of noninclusive practices and make a cohesive and coherent working relationship among the board more likely.[12] Closure, in other words, makes it easier for members to work together. Importantly, it can be improved by means of three practices:[13] *trust*, which fosters efficient coordination and collaboration; *information sharing*, which stimulates openness and learning; and *shared vision*, which reinforces unity of purpose and commitment.

However, reliance on closure may in itself result in group conformity that is counterproductive.[14] Indeed, school board effectiveness is also a function of external ties, or brokerage. While a close-knit working relationship among board members is critical, brokerage is also necessary and is accomplished when members reach outside to others who have new ideas and resources that the group does not have already.[15] Brokerage facilitates alliances among external stakeholders and keeps the board aware of external influences. This allows the board to address issues that lead to uncertainty in the organizational environment. In addition, brokerage helps the board better maintain legitimacy among community stakeholders.[16] For instance, school board relations with state and federal agencies can inform board members about how to deal with competing priorities and help them secure more financial and political support.[17] Ties to civic and advocacy groups and the media provide better community feedback on educational policies and help increase support for the schools.[18] Ties to businesses and universities can be a source of innovative strategies,[19] financial support,[20] and improved curricular and career choices for students.[21]

Figure 3.1 compares school board brokerage with closure. Effective school board performance through improved social capital requires that both closure and brokerage be practiced at high levels. When both are high, the board is most effective and is considered to be practicing *structural autonomy*. Such a board consists of members strongly connected to one another, with extensive relations beyond the group. An autonomous group has productive norms that align people inside the group as well as a strong vision advantage from brokerage outside the group.[22] Its members can form a creative view of valuable projects, know whom to involve, and work together to make it happen.

Research supporting this model comes from studies addressing organizational performance in high-tech industries[23] and the mental health sector,[24] as well as success in cross-functional R&D teams.[25] School board research also provides support for the model. Some of this support is indirect, such as the Lighthouse study, demonstrating how positive changes in members' beliefs and attitudes relate to growth in reading comprehension.[26] Also, Alsbury's work shows that low rates of member turnover (stemming from board cohesiveness and productive board-community connections) relate to higher levels of student achievement.[27] Finally, studies by Saatcioglu et al. and Saatcioglu and Sargut[28] indicate that high levels of brokerage and closure are associated with improvement in student achievement and reduce per pupil expenditures in districts.

Figure 3.1 Matrix comparing closure and brokerage on school boards

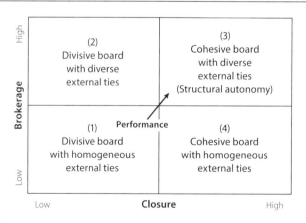

BROKERAGE AND CLOSURE IN PRACTICE: A BALANCED GOVERNANCE APPROACH

The discussion below describes how board members can develop a way to diagnose effective balance of internal working relationship and external ties to develop social capital and help improve district outcomes.

Diagnosing and Promoting Closure

Trust is a vital ingredient for closure in formal task groups, and requires confidence, honesty, and mutual respect. Trust among members facilitates information sharing and shared vision, which align goals and procedures among board members.[29] The instrument shown in table 3.1 below—adapted from Leana and Pil[30]—provides a way for school boards to assess the nature and degree of closure.

Once completed by individual members, scores can be summarized to produce average board scores. There are two important elements in this: the board's average scores for the separate subscales (trust, information sharing, and shared vision), and its grand average score, that is, the average of its three subscale scores. The board's subscale averages provide insights on specific aspects of closure upon which the board can improve. For any given subscale, a board average score of 3.00 (the midpoint of the measurement scale) or above is preferred. A score of 4.00 or above can be treated as a "high" score. Less than 3.00 is a "low" score. Naturally, a board can have a high overall closure score while a specific subscale average is low. However, it may be important to consider ways to improve weaker aspects

Table 3.1   School board closure rating scale

	Strongly agree				Strongly disagree
Trust *Members . . .*					
1. can rely on each other to perform effectively	1	2	3	4	5
2. share a "team spirit"	1	2	3	4	5
3. have confidence in one another	1	2	3	4	5
4. demonstrate a great deal of integrity	1	2	3	4	5

continued

Table 3.1   *continued*

	Strongly agree				Strongly disagree
5. have a relationship built on trust and mutual respect	1	2	3	4	5
6. are sincere in how they relate to one another	1	2	3	4	5
Total:					
Average (divide by six)					

Information sharing
Members . . .

7. engage in open and honest communication with one another	1	2	3	4	5
8. do not have "hidden agendas" or issues	1	2	3	4	5
9. share and accept constructive criticism without making it personal	1	2	3	4	5
10. discuss personal issues if they affect their job responsibilities	1	2	3	4	5
11. willingly share information with one another	1	2	3	4	5
12. keep each other informed all the time	1	2	3	4	5
Total:					
Average (divide by six)					

Shared vision
Members . . .

13. share the same ambitions and vision for the school district	1	2	3	4	5
14. share a common view of the district's purpose in the community	1	2	3	4	5
15. always want to do what's best for the district as a whole	1	2	3	4	5
16. are committed to the goals of the district	1	2	3	4	5
17. view themselves as a partner in charting the direction of the school district	1	2	3	4	5
18. favor the common interests of the district over the interests of any particular group or segment	1	2	3	4	5
Total:					
Average (divide by six)					
Grand average (divide the sum of three averages by three)					

of closure. Subscale averages lower than 3.00 indicate underlying reasons for low levels of closure among board members, and can be used to stimulate the process for cultivating greater closure.

There are multiple ways to improve trust on a school board. First, it is important to address perceptions on how to ensure effective participation and cooperation in board processes and decisions, and on how to improve courteous interaction. Second, board members could identify important topics for members to communicate with one another frequently. Semiformal processes can be established where members inform each other on matters that concern the whole board as well as individual members. Third, members can develop shared norms that demonstrate appreciation for one another along with constructive criticism. Finally, developing common priorities as well as identifying competing ones can improve the level of shared vision on the board. Open discussion on competing and conflicting goals—for the board as a whole and individual members—is a critical first step in constructing a shared vision. Differences about goals can be managed and may become a strength when there is trust and open communication among members. Higher levels of trust and information sharing promote compromises through mutual respect and in light of the interests and future of the district as a whole.

Diagnosing and Promoting Brokerage

Brokerage refers to relations with outside stakeholders, which can foster the board's creativity, diversity, and capability. The instruments shown in table 3.2 and figure 3.2 can be used to evaluate and determine ways to improve brokerage. They identify individual member ties to the outside and offer a means to reflect on how such ties can become more diverse.

Averaging scores from individual members for the brokerage rating scale in table 3.2 can determine the board's score. Unlike the closure scale, the midpoint on the scale is not necessarily a normative reference point for *preferable* scores. While higher brokerage scores are better, members can rely on insights from the instrument in figure 3.2 to determine areas for improvement. This instrument functions as a "name-generator," requiring individual board members to specify names of stakeholders they know and/or have ties to that can influence the board's operations.

Table 3.2   School board brokerage rating scale

How frequently do you interact with individuals in the following groups?	Never				Daily
1. Local business leaders	1	2	3	4	5
2. State legislators	1	2	3	4	5
3. Local municipal government officials	1	2	3	4	5
4. PTO/PTA leaders	1	2	3	4	5
5. Civic community leaders	1	2	3	4	5
6. Faith community leaders	1	2	3	4	5
7. Ethnic/minority group representatives	1	2	3	4	5
8. Seniors/retirees	1	2	3	4	5
9. News/media representatives	1	2	3	4	5
10. Youth group leaders	1	2	3	4	5
11. Leaders in higher education	1	2	3	4	5
12. Officials from other school districts	1	2	3	4	5
13. Other … please specify:	1	2	3	4	5
14. Other … please specify:	1	2	3	4	5
15. Other … please specify:	1	2	3	4	5

At any given level (district, state, and local), stakeholder names can be generated associated with any category addressed in table 3.2 (business leaders, universities, legislature, etc.). These names can then be combined for the entire board.

Members can focus on two particular issues for improving the board's overall brokerage. First, *redundancies* can be assessed by developing a list of common ties to external stakeholders. An external stakeholder known by every member on the board is an example of redundancy. While redundancies are inevitable, *and at times necessary*, redundancy should be at a moderate level, such that the average external stakeholder with ties to the board should *not* be known by more than 25–50 percent of the board members. Boards with higher redundancy scores for a majority of their external ties should try to reduce this by individual members developing new, nonredundant ties in their community through networking and outreach

Figure 3.2 Name-generator tool for cultivating school board

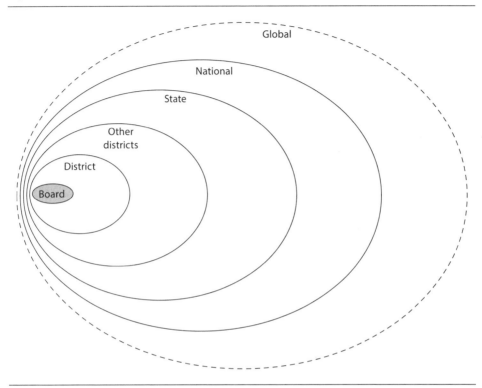

efforts. This strategy can improve overall brokerage for the board without compromising existing external ties.

The second important issue on which to focus is the *quality* of external ties. A tie in itself may not be beneficial if it is not positive. Members of the board can reflect on how to change the nature of unproductive and/or adverse ties. This requires renegotiation or recasting of such contacts. It may involve tie transfers, where a negative tie for a given member can be recultivated by fellow board members in a new light. Insights from the name-generator tool are useful for the board to identify levels (district, state, national) and/or categories (business leaders, universities, legislature, etc.) of external ties that the board lacks as a whole. For example, if nobody on the board has productive ties to state policy makers, experts, or leaders, then members can develop strategies to create such ties.

CONCLUSION

School boards have historically lacked significant attention in education research and practice.[31] This is changing, given the growing interest in examining boards and improving them. Contemporary work on school boards is transpiring in the age of accountability, which makes it important to develop theories of board functioning and strategies for effectiveness in relationship to concrete results, such as student achievement and more efficient use of district resources. Building social capital on boards through balancing closure and brokerage offers a promising approach to enhance school governance. The model and practical tools in this chapter facilitate boards' efforts to evaluate and improve their effectiveness in ways that can make an important difference in district outcomes.

4

How Board Governance Practices Affect Student Achievement

Ivan J. Lorentzen and William P. McCaw

School boards hear it all the time: "Do what's best for students." It's easy to say, but surprisingly hard to accomplish. Boards often find themselves entangled in issues detached from this simple ideal and lose sight of the fact that schools exist to benefit students. Helping school boards govern the district in a balanced manner known to promote student achievement is the subject of this chapter.

There is an unacceptably wide disparity in student achievement across school districts. While some districts' students excel, others report low achievement. Since the public expects schools to educate students for their successful future, boards need to know which of their actions and decisions serve to improve a student's likelihood of success and which interfere with the student's education.

Numerous organizations use some variation of a board to help achieve the organizational mission. Banks, corporations, churches, symphonies, and the military all rely on the collective expertise of boards to advance their causes. Boards provide significant benefit when members are selected based on personal expertise or demonstrated proficiency. However, in public education, this is not always the case. School board members come from all walks of life and are selected for many reasons. According to Maeroff, "Most school boards are filled with citizen volunteers who lack expertise beyond the source of their livelihoods."[1] Without specific expertise and guidance, board members rely on good intentions, campaign promises, intuition, or personal preference to drive their actions. This leaves citizen-controlled public education in jeopardy of becoming an assortment of novel individual efforts detached from the educational enterprise and subject to change with each new member elected to the board. It doesn't have to be this way.

BACKGROUND

In 2002, No Child Left Behind was signed into law and student achievement became the new mission of public education.[2] Already saddled with traditional duties like budget, policy, and community relations, school boards across America were confronted with the additional responsibility of raising student achievement. There were many ideas as to how a board was to accomplish this; the problem was that no one really knew how board actions were related to student achievement.

While teachers and administrators have relied on research-based advice to increase student achievement, boards had little comparable research to consult. Previous studies suggested that school boards in districts with high student achievement behave differently than boards in districts with low student achievement.[3] The research discussed in this chapter extends these earlier studies and explores the relationship between board actions and student achievement. This relationship is now described in more detail.[4]

Critics have long asserted that school boards are irrelevant to improving student performance. However, claiming that the actions and behaviors of school boards have no impact on student achievement is indefensible in light of recent research.[5] Therefore, it is the duty of school board members to recognize and understand their influence in supporting student learning. The actions boards take, or fail to take, combined with the issues they choose to address, affect the entire school district. When the political or personal motivation of a board member trumps the larger educational concern, or when the board fails to provide suitable leadership and governance, student achievement can be harmed.[6] However, when the board acts appropriately, students benefit.

The effect of a school board on student achievement is indirect and several layers removed from the student. If a school district is to seriously pursue its educational mission, it is vital that boards recognize their role: "to focus on student achievement as their primary responsibility."[7] Board decisions affect the working conditions in schools, which, in turn, influence student achievement. It is recommended that boards conduct annual self-assessments to assist them in creating environments related to high student achievement. Board self-assessments examine appropriate actions and roles of boards and superintendents. When boards stay focused at the policy level, administrators are better able to manage and lead the district, allowing teachers to focus on the education of students.[8] There is now a diagnostic self-assessment tool that can assist boards achieve Balanced Governance.

The Washington State School Board Standards

The Board Self-Assessment Survey (BSAS) was an outgrowth of the Washington State School Board Standards Task Force and was guided by three comprehensive reports and research efforts. Waters and Marzano of the Mid-continent Research for Education and Learning (McREL)[9] conducted several studies, and others were part of the Lighthouse Inquiry conducted by the Iowa Association of School Boards.[10] The third was from the National School Board Association's *Key Works of School Boards* by Gemberling, Smith, and Villani.[11] From these reports and research, the task force identified and verified five essential principles, or board standards, thought to be related to student achievement. These became known as "The School Board Standards."[12]

Each of these five standards is measured by the BSAS. The first requires that boards provide responsible school governance. The second asks boards to set and communicate high expectations for student learning with clear goals and plans for meeting those expectations. The third calls for the creation of conditions districtwide for student and staff success. The fourth involves holding the district accountable for meeting student learning expectations. Finally, the fifth entails engaging the local community in order to represent the values and expectations they hold for their schools. These standards describe critical areas of board performance.

The Montana Study—What Is Known

Research conducted in Montana in 2013, called the Board Governance and Student Achievement Study, demonstrates which specific board actions were related to high student achievement.[13] This study utilized the BSAS to assess board best practice (hereafter referred to as boardsmanship). Self-assessment ratings for each board were compared with their district's tenth-grade student achievement scores measured by the Montana Criterion Reference Test in math, reading, and science. While the statistical predictability of the findings are specific to Montana, these findings are relevant to other school boards in their quest to increase student achievement.

Relationships Between Boards and Student Achievement. The Montana study found that all five board standards identified as critical in the study were associated with high student achievement at a statistically significant level.[14] This study prioritized the elements of effective boardsmanship by providing specific recommendations for boards to follow. In particular, school boards can embrace the following seven elements of effective boardsmanship contained within the standards. These seven prioritized elements represent a Balanced Governance approach to board practice.

First, effective boards hold the school district accountable for meeting student learning expectations by evaluating the superintendent on clear and focused expectations. To accomplish this, boards commit to the following three actions: creating written goals for the superintendent focused on specific outcomes for student learning; communicating performance expectations for the superintendent to the community; and basing decisions regarding the superintendent's contract on objective evaluation of their performance on student achievement goals.

Second, boards set and communicate high expectations for student learning with clear goals and plans for meeting those expectations. Boards that effectively address this second element adopt a collaboratively developed district plan focused on learning and achievement outcomes for all students. A well-developed plan involves collaborating with staff and the community to formulate and maintain a district plan with goals and outcomes. In addition, the board bases its ongoing work, such as policy development, decision making, and budgeting, on these district goals. The board also continually monitors progress toward the goals and outcomes of the district plan.

Third, the board has an obligation to commit to a continuous improvement plan regarding student achievement at each school and throughout the district.

Continuous improvement begins when the district follows a schedule for the timely review of the district plan. Coherence between the district plan and school improvement plan is important. Therefore, it is critical that the board annually review and make recommendations to these plans.

Fourth, the board provides responsible school district governance by conducting board and district business in a fair, respectful, and responsible manner. This is accomplished when the board commits to a clear and shared purpose.

Fifth, the board engages the local community and represents the values and expectations the community holds for its schools. This is accomplished by soliciting input from staff and a wide spectrum of the community. By listening to these groups, boards are able to consider a diverse range of interests and perspectives in their decision making to gain community and staff support.

Sixth, the board models responsible school district governance by working as an effective and collaborative team. Effective boards work with the superintendent to establish a commitment to student achievement. In addition, the board pursues individual and collective professional development to improve board members' knowledge and skills by attending conferences and holding study sessions. Finally, the effective board uses a collaborative processes that results in well-informed problem solving and decision-making.

The seventh and last element of effective boardsmanship requires the board to create districtwide conditions for student and staff success. This can be accomplished by providing for learning essentials, including rigorous curricula, technology, and high-quality facilities. Boards need to adopt a process that includes community and parent involvement in developing curricula. In addition, effective boards create policy that requires rigorous and regular evaluation of curricula and supplemental materials to ensure that they align with state and district standards. A process to support the evaluation and updating of technology is necessary, as well as the development of a long-term facilities plan for construction and maintenance. These seven elements are the essentials of effective boardsmanship.

Boards in Disarray.   Student achievement was found to be lower in those districts where individual board members reported broad disagreement over essential elements of effective boardsmanship described above. A board exhibiting broad disagreement may be a board in *disarray*. Empirical evidence indicates that a more collaborative board governs a smoother functioning district, which is associated with higher student achievement. These conclusions offer compelling justification for board members to seek agreement on elements of boardsmanship and governance for the good of the students in their district. Research supports the link between board conflict and lowering student achievement. The Board Governance and Student Achievement Study provided unique data noting that board consensus (i.e., collaboration) on issues of governance plays an important role in achievement scores in Montana.[15]

Boards that experience conflict and disarray destabilize district efforts designed to raise achievement. When poor student achievement occurs in a district, boards need to examine their own actions and understand the influence these actions have on student success. A Balanced Governance approach combines efforts to address internal governance disagreements (i.e., reduce disarray) while focusing on the seven elements of effective boardsmanship described above. Doing so may reduce the meddling in administrative and management issues. Such meddling upsets delicate relationships, frustrates administrators and staff, leads to district-wide strife, and can be associated with student achievement decline.[16]

What Does This Mean for School Boards?

The actions of school boards matter. The board has a duty to embrace the board standards, namely, to provide responsible governance (i.e., reduce disarray), set high expectations for student learning, create the conditions districtwide for student and staff success, hold the teachers and administrators accountable for student success, and engage the local community.[17] If the board fails to address these critical tasks or fails to understand that these issues comprise their primary responsibilities, the district will be lacking an important contribution to student success.

Without an understanding of a Balanced Governance approach, supported by these standards, boards can experience mission drift and begin assuming duties of the superintendent while failing to realize the negative impact on staff and students. As Goodman and Zimmerman put it, "When board members and superintendents are unclear about who is responsible for what duties, conflict, inefficiency, and frustration are inevitable."[18] Assuming administrative duties by the board is an all-too-common scenario, which has undesirable impacts on the school district. But if boards work toward a Balanced Governance approach, they will carry out their essential duties by governing the district in a manner most conducive to student success.

Balanced Governance is a choice. By following the principles of effective boardsmanship described in the board standards, school boards can join the efforts of parents, teachers, principals, and superintendents aimed at raising student achievement. If student achievement is to continue improving as schools respond to mandates for school reform, all relevant factors must be identified, employed, and aligned in support of this goal.

Only the Board.   Before a district can effectively address low student achievement, the school board needs to establish the districtwide conditions conducive for improvement. Properly engaged school boards are essential to school improvement, and a core measure of school improvement is student achievement. The relationship between effective boardsmanship and student achievement has been established. While the association is admittedly indirect, the relationship is real.

Being a valuable member of an effective school board that governs a thriving school district is challenging, but it can be done. Members who think it can't be done in their district need to examine turn-around schools and the critical role played by the school board.[19] And those who think student achievement is the sole job of the teachers or administration need to better understand Balanced Governance and the elements of effective boardsmanship.

School boards today can work in a balanced way by adhering to actions known to promote student achievement while dropping harmful personal agendas and counterproductive initiatives. Embracing elements of Balanced Governance is not, in itself, a guarantee of immediate district success and improved student improvement, but members who take this approach are at least focused on the right things and will begin to think, behave, and act like an effective Balanced Governance board that governs a thriving district with high achieving students.

What Is a Board to Do?

The level of excellence in a district is affected by the school board's ability to work together as a team, set visible standards of excellence, and effectively govern the district. School board members have no excuse to remain uninformed about issues of governance and boardsmanship related to student achievement. At the end of the day, the function of a school board is to govern the district from the mezzanine and attend to the most vital aspects of Balanced Governance.

For some boards, embracing these aspects requires shifting their focus. Some issues previously thought to be within the purview of the board need to be referred to the administration. Other issues previously thought of as less important come into focus. If changes such as these are to occur, they must begin with boards, and they must happen on two fronts—first with the individual school board member, and second with the collective board. This two-pronged approach to improving school governance, and ultimately student achievement, is what constitutes improved, focused, and effective boardsmanship. Both of these elements, along with the tools to accomplish them, are presented within this book and constitute a primary element of a Balanced Governance approach. In addition, as noted below, the relationship of the board with the community is of key importance, as is its relationship with the superintendent.

The Individual Board Member. How does one become a productive board member and develop effective boardsmanship? First, there are a few things board members should *not* do. Effective boardsmanship is *not* an entitlement to do anything you wish once elected to the board. Despite promises made, you are not suddenly a hired educator or administrator. Second, effective boardsmanship is *not* sitting back, deferring to the administration, and letting the district fend for itself. This is clearly an abdication of duty. And last, effective boardsmanship is *not* making impossible and unrealistic demands on district administrators and teachers regarding student achievement. Making unrealistic demands ensures failure to affect long term changes to the district.

Effective boardsmanship is, however, a specific set of characteristics, skills, abilities, perceptions, and competencies of board members modeled in the Balanced Governance approach and described in the Board Standards. For some, this may require more collaboration with fellow board members. For others it may require a change in attention. Paul Houston advises school leaders to avoid the "killer B's," which include spending too much time focused on things like buses, buildings, books, budgets, ballgames, and bonds. If you concentrate on the B's, you're spending too much time off task. Instead, focus on the "critical C's" such as connections, communication, collaboration, community building, child advocacy, and curricular choices.[20] The C's constitute the heart of what board members should be focused on. To see if you or your board is focused on the B's or C's, examine the minutes and agendas of your meetings for the past year or two and tally the topics that captured your time and attention. This exercise can be very revealing and can prompt a change in individual and collective focus.

The Collective Board.   Primarily, the collective board should make a long-term commitment to becoming a governing body modeling the Balanced Governance approach and applying effective boardsmanship elements. Second, the board should recognize they do not exist in isolation. The board operates in a delicately balanced relationship with the community and with the superintendent. These relationships must be constantly nurtured and can be viewed as each entity having separate but overlapping roles. Understanding how these roles interact is important as schools seek to structure themselves for the benefit of students.

The appropriate balance of "separate but overlapping" roles appears simple enough, but this is not the case given the complex nature of the relationships. Achieving the appropriate amount of overlap is critical in order to accomplish Balanced Governance. While the exact extent of the overlap cannot be described in detail because no supporting data is known to exist, figure 4.1 provides a visual for

Figure 4.1   Balanced relationships between board and community, and board and superintendent

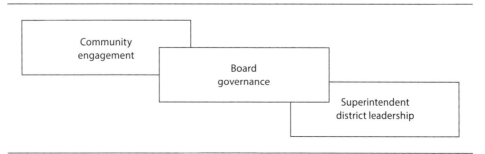

boards to consider when determining the extent to which the board interacts with both the superintendent and the community.

Relationship with the Community.   Only the community can do some things, while only the board can do others. However, there are some things on which the board and community need to collaborate. The interaction and collaboration between the board and community is an ongoing relationship that must be nurtured and sustained for the sake of students. Schools need to be a reflection of the communities in which they serve. The school board is responsible for assisting the community in understanding the current realities of public education, as well as listening to the community to see what type of schools the community wants and is willing to support. This will entail a sustained and continuous effort involving both formal and informal interactions with parents, educators, legislators, community leaders, and the public in general. Learning how to simultaneously lead and follow the community is a challenge for every board. When it's done skillfully, the school district can expect continuing and robust public support.

Relationship with the Superintendent.   Again, there are some things only the board can do, others that can only be done by the superintendent, and some that require the collaboration of both parties. As illustrated in figure 4.2, too little overlap between the board and superintendent can lead to excessive deference by the board to the superintendent—that is, rubber-stamping—which is an abdication of duty. On the other hand, too much overlap can result in micromanagement—a poisonous overreach of board responsibilities.

These relationships are highly contextual and complex. It is only through an understanding of the nuances of these relationships that boards can come to collective agreement on the amount of appropriate overlap in order to establish and maintain Balanced Governance.

Boards and superintendents must work to establish the nature of their roles. When respective duties and responsibilities are appropriate and clearly delineated, the superintendent and school board both benefit. Selection and evaluation of a capable leader of the school district was the top scoring item in the Board Governance and Student Achievement Study completed in 2013.[21]

Figure 4.2   Two examples of boards out of balance

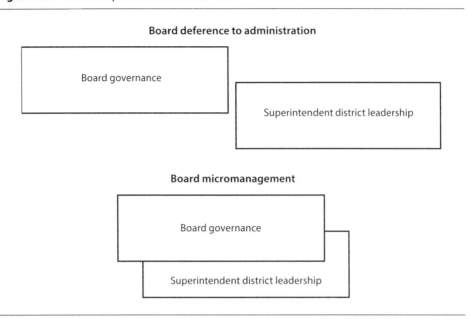

One of the school board's foremost responsibilities is to attract, hire, support, and retain an effective educational leader. Frequent superintendent turnover effectively guarantees failed long-term efforts to improve the district resulting in lower student achievement.[22] Together with the community and staff, the board and superintendent need to carve out a long-term educational plan designed to improve student achievement. To do so requires the time, training, and resources needed to accomplish the goals. Progress needs to be measured accurately and readjusted when necessary.

CONCLUSION

High student achievement is the final measure of success for any school, and school boards have an important role to play. Empirical evidence describes the relationship between boardsmanship and student achievement, and this evidence can be used to guide board actions. Since school boards now have research that describes practices related to student achievement, boards can no longer hold teachers and administrators solely accountable for poor performance.

School boards also have a duty to govern the district properly by practicing a Balanced Governance approach, which includes effective boardsmanship, both individually and collectively, as articulated by the board standards. Along with administrators, teachers, and the community, effective school boards share in the responsibility for student achievement. Ultimately, the system either promotes or hinders student achievement.[23] This necessitates effective board participation in districtwide efforts related to high student achievement. There can be no honest objection to raising student achievement by improving the capacity of school boards and their members.

PART II

Putting Balanced Governance to Work

5

What School Board
Members Need to Know

Assessing Leadership

Mark Levine and Paul Van Buskirk

INTRODUCTION

This chapter reports on research into effective school board behaviors and describes a new district-level school board leadership assessment; a Balanced Governance tool that associates specific governance practices with student performance. Importantly, it demonstrates higher levels of student achievement test scores in school districts where board members collectively scored higher on the MHL assessment—a school board assessment tool described later in this chapter. This supports our premise that school boards that knowingly or unknowingly practice a Balanced Governance model report higher student achievement scores on their state's achievement tests.

This is important because a review of the literature on school governance and student achievement, including decades of performance-based educational reform in the United States, reveals several key findings:

- Increased attention continues to be focused on school board accountability and its impact on student performance.[1]

- Student achievement is the ultimate measure of educational value.[2]
- School districts nationwide continue to struggle to raise student achievement and narrow achievement gaps.[3]
- Although there continues to be a need for quantitative research and practical tools to help board members raise student achievement, these resources remain scarce or limited.[4]

Literature on school board research is rife with conclusions and recommendations based on personal experience, observations, opinions, and anecdotal evidence rather than carefully designed studies.[5] This is supported by Delagardelle's finding that opinion-based writings on the role of school boards and student achievement dominate the literature.[6] Further, Walser perceived that research remains essentially descriptive and lacks a systematic examination of how governance relates to outcomes.[7] The need to identify effective school board assessments and training tools is a national issue. Districts are held increasingly responsible for improving student achievement.

This chapter provides an overview of the MHL research[8] along with practical tools to help school board members improve student achievement. The research establishes a relationship between the behaviors of school board members and student achievement within a Balanced Governance model. This multistate study and the MHL assessment were designed to address the scarcity of resources available to help school board members raise student achievement. This is accomplished through twenty-one specific and highly regarded research findings and a practical training program entitled Empowering, which includes six modules and the use of the MHL assessment tool. The MHL assessment survey was designed for the following purposes:

- To explore and explain board members' beliefs and actions that result in high student performance
- To demonstrate that high scores on the MHL school board assessment tool in leadership skills, governance, and community relations link to higher student achievement
- To provide an effective, research-supported training tool for board members

- To support a Balanced Governance model, where each board member shares the leadership responsibilities

Drawing from years of experience in human resource and development (HRD) and research on school governance and student achievement, our study was guided by the goal to enhance learning and improve an organization's performance.[9]

A review of the literature, as it relates to organizations, education, and performance through an HRD perspective, reveals that

- school boards, like any board of directors, serve as the elected or appointed leadership accountable to their stakeholders for their organization's performance[10] and are responsible to provide the education the community expects;[11]
- the success of an organization depends on the quality of the product it produces—in this case student achievement;[12] and
- leadership is most effective when board members transcend the factors that have adverse effects on their duties and decisions (for example, personal ambition, a political agenda, inability to work together).[13]

LINKING SCHOOL GOVERNANCE TO STUDENT ACHIEVEMENT: THE STUDY

In the MHL study, data were collected from the school board members of a school district that had the highest student achievement scores in a state highly regarded for improving student achievement. In our case study, five board members were selected to participate because their school district had the highest percentage of A- and B-rated schools and the highest percent of level 3, 4, and 5 composite scores on the state exam in reading, math, and writing during the 2004–2005 school year.

Information was collected through interviews with the board members to explore their experiences and perspectives about school governance and how it might predict successful student performance (achievement). Some open-ended questions were:

- What is unique about your board's way of working that has resulted in such high levels of student achievement in your school district?

- How do five elected board members with different values and backgrounds work together to make a school board decision that will raise student achievement?
- In your opinion, what is the most important decision your board has made that contributed to your school district's high student achievement?
- What governance conditions are necessary to raise students' achievement?

The results were that leadership, community relations, and governance (as predictors) were associated with high student scores (performance outcomes).

DEVELOPING THE MHL ASSESSMENT TOOL

One outcome of the study was the development of the MHL school board assessment, as a way to measure the relationship between the governance predictors shown in figure 5.1 and their students' test scores (achievement). The MHL school board leadership assessment uses seven or eight questions developed for each of the governance predictors: leadership, community relations, and governance style. A sample question for the governance style predictor is:

> How effectively does your oversight of the school district's academic performance provide you with the information you need to allocate district resources to raise achievement?

The MHL school board leadership assessment was tested for content validity and piloted with thirty school board members and found to meet statistical criteria for reliability and validity. The school board leadership assessment was applied statewide to school board members across different states with the same results.

Figure 5.1   Governance predictors associated with high student scores

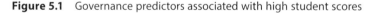
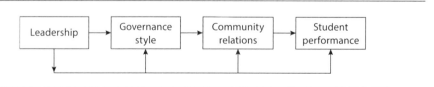

What We Learned About Effective Board Governance

As a result of multistate studies, the following school governance and student achievement findings can help board members and educational leaders nationwide govern effectively to raise student achievement.

1. Regardless of whether school boards knowingly or unknowingly apply a Balanced Governance model, their success in raising student achievement is dependent on Balanced Governance behavior like shared leadership and decision making.
2. School boards whose members score high on the MHL assessment in leadership, governance style, and community relations are associated with high district student achievement test scores.
3. The MHL assessment results in similar positive benefits for school boards regardless of location or size and can be used as part of a district self-assessment training tool.
4. Twenty-one governance predictors, associated with leadership, governance style, and community relations on the MHL assessment, relate to raising student achievement. For example, in the category of governance style, the board's oversight of the school district's academic performance links to raising student achievement.

Describing Empowering As a School Board Training Program

One outcome of the studies noted above was the ability to use the results of the MHL assessment tool and design an effective school board training program to improve student achievement. The training program is organized into six sequential modules or a series of interventions that describe how school board members can operate to improve student achievement and other district goals. The modules are described in the sections below.

Module 1.   School board members, as a group, may self-administer the MHL leadership assessment survey and (a) compare, analyze, and discuss their individual and collective scores on the leadership, governance style, and community relations categories, (b) determine their individual and collective strengths, weaknesses, and needs, and (c) use these results as a baseline to monitor and assess progress on an annual intervention plan to raise student achievement. The assessment may be readministered throughout the school year to measure the board's progress.

Module 2. School board members participate in a short course with the curriculum focused on shared leadership. During the course, board members as a group demonstrate in writing how their intervention plan to raise achievement applies the Balanced Governance Model. This same process applies to board members who do not have an intervention plan. For example:

> Balanced Governance can be used to address leadership issues (i.e., fiscal, legal, policy, and educational issues) that are aligned with their expertise and organizational role and goals.

Module 3. This module is based on the Bevino report—a case study of a designed plan to turn around a school district from 2001 through 2005. The report chronicles the interventions taken by this district's board and administration in response to their community's dissatisfaction with students' performance, operations, and communication.[14] As part of Module 3, school board members as a group analyze and discuss the report, then list and discuss ten interventions they believe their own district can implement to improve achievement.

The Bevino report demonstrates that a board with high student achievement practices a Balanced Governance model. It reveals that the district being studied began its transformation when the board and administration developed goals and specific plans to (a) increase student achievement, (b) make resource decisions based on student needs, and (c) improve communication with parents and the community. As a result, the district rose from twenty-seventh place in student achievement in 2001 to first in the state in 2004–2005. Excitingly, the district continues to place among the top six districts in their state in student achievement.

Bevino describes how the academic and organizational transformation focused the district's attention on student achievement. Based on their understanding that those closest to the students are the most knowledgeable and responsible for student achievement, the board and administration implemented significant organizational and academic changes, including:

- the decentralization of financial and instructional authority to the schools;
- downsizing district departments, allocating 91 percent of yearly FTE dollars to the schools and reducing district overhead costs to 9 percent;
- making financial decisions based on students' academic needs;
- promoting parent responsibility and involvement;
- implementing strategies to differentiate and individualize instruction;
- using research-proven, most-effective teaching methods;
- predicting and evaluating school work on results, not process; and
- reassigning district personnel to schools for direct support.

The comprehensive intervention plan demonstrates how the district's culture changed, calling for teachers who know how to teach, leaders who know the work of teachers, and effective administrators. Effective administrators are those who can evaluate the teaching in their school, analyze student data to make instructional decisions that increase achievement, and allocate resources that support those decisions. Collectively, these plans meant that the board, superintendent, and principals must provide the resources, clarity, and training needed to make the change successful.

This case study of the district's turnaround is congruent with research on school governance that exemplifies a Balanced Governance approach. Although school districts have their own culture and challenges, the Bevino report provides an effective tool to develop and implement a comprehensive plan to raise student achievement. The interventions presented only represent a sample of the extensive intervention plan administered.

Module 4. School board members may participate in a group discussion related to the research questions used in the Bevino Report case study and the interventions that resulted in improvements in student achievement. If there are multiple district boards participating, they may take part in a group discussion with board members from other districts. Examples of discussion questions include:

- How has your board affected high levels of student achievement in your district?

- How does your board work together to make school board decisions?

A facilitated question-and-answer session should follow.

Module 5. Role playing or role training is an activity in which board members assume a role and review and rehearse real school board scenarios to improve their content and shared leadership, problem solving, and communication skills. A board member can view problems and solutions from different perspectives. The following is an example of steps for a role-playing or role-training session:

- The facilitator introduces the scenario or problem and encourages open discussion of issues. For example, how can a board formulate district goals and objectives to achieve higher student achievement?
- Provide a clear picture of the scenario. For example, establish a benchmark to (a) measure student achievement, (b) measure future progress, and (c) assess what members are expected to achieve at the end of the session.
- Identify the role each member will play. For example, one member will provide leadership for fiscal matters and financial analysis. Another may provide leadership in legal matters. Another may lead community relations and define roles in a shared leadership model.
- Members can develop a series of strategies to achieve goals and objectives that improve student achievement. When finished with the session, members can discuss what they learned and their strengths and weaknesses.

Module 6. School board members review and analyze responses to community relations questions on the MHL assessment that resulted in low to moderate relationships between the community relation construct and raising student performance (achievement). School board members may want to first review and analyze their community relations program throughout the school year, and then use these reviews as a baseline to monitor and assess their strengths, weaknesses, and progress to ensure their program helps raise student achievement. For example, if the district does not have a community relations program it should develop one and follow the above process. During this module, board members, as a group, develop or revise their community relations program and develop goals and objectives to improve student achievement.

CONCLUSION

The MHL assessment can empower school board leaders to improve their governance skills and raise student achievement. This study and the assessment tool demonstrate that successful school board members (a) administer prudent businesslike governance and leadership practices, (b) transcend personal and systemic counterproductive and self-serving governance behavior, and (c) focus their talents and resources on realistic solutions to raise student achievement. Effective board leaders understand that their success, as well as their students', depends on their productive shared leadership and decision making as exemplified in Balanced Governance.

6

Elements of School Board Success

A Comprehensive Board Assessment Tool
for Systemic Improvement

Thomas L. Alsbury and Betsy Miller-Jones

School board members bring a variety of backgrounds and understanding of the governance role to their work. For decades, board leadership has been characterized as hiring the best superintendent possible, then hoping that their leadership, together with the board members' community-based information and knowledge, will lead to good decision making for the local schools and community. Over time, however, research has identified good practices, and structures, that help to make boards more effective with more probable success in leading improved school performance.

Some of the most frequently seen bumps in the road of this leadership model include a difference of expectations of who does what, and miscommunication between the two roles of the board and superintendent, including what should be communicated and how. The Oregon School Boards Association took a look at the research available, along with their own experience working one-on-one with boards and superintendents—both those in distress and those functioning at a high level—in order to put together a road map for success.

The result was the development of a set of standards known as Elements of Success, representing the characteristics of highly effective school boards (see figure 6.1). But more than just a list of what is, or might be, the elements provide boards with a launch pad for how they can become more successful. The elements can be used as an evaluation document, a foundation for discussion, and most importantly, a map for action.

As shown in figure 6.1, the ten elements are broken into two categories: technical and adaptive. Technical elements relate to areas where there exists a considerable body of practical knowledge and experience along with in-service training programs. Numerous sets of board standards and evaluation instruments include these general topics. Boards (or some members of the board) may have sufficient knowledge related to the technical elements already, but the board may need assistance with systemic implementation or the application of the research, experience, or training programs in new and better ways. Technical elements include forming a vision for the district, effective leadership, community engagement, using data, and providing accountability.

Adaptive elements are more complex, beyond what we typically already know, and will often take much longer to implement. Adaptive elements usually require that the entire system adapt in ways that may be unfamiliar or uncomfortable at first. They apply when there is a gap between aspiration and reality or where there is limited research or knowledge about how to implement change in the district. As such, they often demand a response outside the board's current repertoire and may require some difficult new learning. Adaptive elements include systems thinking, becoming a learning organization, cultural competence, climate, and innovation and creativity.

ELEMENTS OF SUCCESS COMPARED TO TRADITIONAL BOARD STANDARDS

School board members may well wonder how the Elements of Success differ from the board standards they have seen in the past. First, the Elements of Success include ten characteristics of highly successful boards, with five of the elements not commonly found in other board standards, namely the adaptive elements. Second, even when the characteristics in lists of other board standards match or seem to match, the Elements of Success tend to differ in the focus of their intent, as shown

Figure 6.1   Elements of success: School board standards and characteristics found in highly effective school boards

Technical Elements

ELEMENT #1 Vision-Directed Planning. Boards engage communities and staff in the development of a shared vision focused on student learning. The vision is the foundation of the mission and sets goals that direct board policy making, planning, resource allocation, and activities.

ELEMENT #2 Community Engagement. All members of the community are stakeholders in the success of their schools. Community engagement is a reciprocal advocacy process that creates and sustains meaningful conversations, systems connections, and feedback loops with all groups in the community. Successful community engagement results in collaborative partnerships and new types and levels of community participation in schools.

ELEMENT #3 Effective Leadership. Board leadership is proactive, integrated, and distributed. Boards establish focus, direction, and expectations that foster student learning. Across the district, boards develop and implement collaborative leadership models and practices that are guided by shared student learning goals. Within the district, boards align authority and responsibility so decisions can be made at levels close to implementation.

ELEMENT #4 Accountability. Boards have high expectations for the learning of all students and hold themselves and their organizations accountable for reaching those results. Boards align policy, resource allocation, staffing, curriculum, professional development, and other activities with the vision and goals for student learning. The accountability process includes recognition of successes and support where improvement is needed.

ELEMENT #5 Using Data for Continuous Improvement. Continuous improvement is the antithesis of complacency. Boards use data and information, from multiple sources and in various formats, to identify areas for improvement, set priorities, and monitor improvement efforts. At the same time, they seek even better ways to do things the organization is already doing well.

Adaptive Elements

ELEMENT #6 Cultural Responsiveness. The cultural diversity of a community has many facets—social, economic, political, religious, geographical, generational, linguistic, ethnic, racial, and gender. Boards develop an understanding of this diversity and uphold perspectives that reflect the cultures in their community. Effective community engagement and expectancy strategies build on the strengths of a community's cultural diversity.

ELEMENT #7 Climate. Boards create a climate of the expectations that all students can learn at high levels. Board policy making and activities foster a positive and safe learning climate that supports the vision for student learning. The board models professional relationships and a culture of mutual respect.

ELEMENT #8 Learning Organizations. A learning organization is a self-renewing professional community that supports reflection, discovery, learning, improvement, and success by staff at all levels. Boards encourage professional development that empowers staff and nurtures leadership capacity across the organization.

ELEMENT #9 Systems Thinking. Systems thinking allows boards to break out of the box of single district thinking and act on an integrated view of education within and across systems and levels (e.g., K–12, ESD, community college, and university). Boards that practice systems thinking open the door for collaborative local, state, and national partnerships, coordinated programs, and shared resource models to improve student learning.

ELEMENT #10 Innovation and Creativity. Innovation and creativity are assets to the process of development and change, leading to new types of thinking and better ways of meeting student needs. Innovation and creativity are not predictable, but can flourish when boards align vision throughout the organization, engage in collaborative partnerships, and encourage dialogue, new ideas, and differing perspectives.

in important differences in wording or emphasis. Some of these differences are discussed in the following sections.

Vision-Directed Planning

While most lists of effectiveness standards include the importance of a board vision, the details in how this standard is expressed can differ. Vision-Directed Planning describes the more general evaluation of the process of visioning for student learning. Terms used in this element include "engaging community and staff" and "shared vision," noting the importance of involving internal and external stakeholders in the visioning process. The element reflects research support of a collaboratively developed vision.

Another unique descriptor in this element is the use of the term "student learning" compared to the current popular trend to use terms like "student achievement." While this may seem like a minor difference, it is in fact critically important. Using "achievement" restricts success to student test scores. "Student learning" provides a much broader and more research-supported standard. Boards adopting the element of Vision-Directed Planning understand that the rise in the scores in sixth-grade math on a particular standardized test do not necessarily indicate individual or even overall student growth in learning.

Finally, the element makes a critical addition by linking vision, mission, and goals to policy, resource allocation, and activities. It is important that the board not only hold high expectations for student learning but that it ensure that every policy and resource decision be assessed on whether they support that vision. Unfortunately, some underperforming boards have adopted a high achievement, high accountability vision but then use that standard to support punitive policy, criticism of teachers, and justification for intrusion into management and personnel decisions in the district. The additional language in the element helps define the role of the board as monitoring its own level of success in aligning resources, policy, and procedure to the vision. This helps keep the board focused on its appropriate role of balanced governance and avoiding micromanagement.

Community Engagement

Most boards include a goal involving community relations. However, this standard is often poorly defined. Community relations should clarify what that relationship should include, who is involved, or how that relationship is maintained. Indeed, a focus on "strong communications" with the staff and the community, primarily to "inform" them on what the district has decided to do and how the community can support that decision, is not enough. The language in this element is intentional in noting the need to involve "all" members of the community. In addition, this element focuses on the concept of "reciprocal advocacy" to create and sustain not only "meaningful" conversation, but "system connections" and "feedback loops." School boards often believe that if they publish a newsletter, open their meetings up to public comment, and place a parent or two on school committees that they have fulfilled the standard of community relations.

The language in this element makes the goal to enact deep and meaningful changes in the school-community relationship and focuses on proactive dialogue over reactive communication. The proof of the importance of this difference can be seen in the decision in most districts to employ professional communications directors as the mouthpiece for the district. This element speaks to authentic and organic two-way engagement, not filtered antiseptic talking points provided by a professional communicator who is an expert at political spin. Boards hoping to achieve this element attend to much deeper and more relevant evaluation of their school system connections and feedback loops.

Effective Leadership

This element provides another example of a unique board standard. First, most boards focus only on the work done by their members and/or with the superintendent when considering issues of leadership. The element expands the responsibility of the school board to ensure that the policies they approve and the criteria in which they evaluate the superintendent include an assessment of whether leadership "throughout the district" is "proactive," "integrated," and "distributed." Further, this element sets a standard for the board to expect leadership to align authority and responsibilities so that decisions can be made at the levels closest to implementation. In practical terms, this element discourages the use of mandates from the central office or the school board and encourages the development of solutions by teachers and those personnel who best understand the problems and how to develop and implement workable solutions. While this element does not support any form of micromanagement, it presses the school board to adopt a vision that includes ensuring that the district distribute leadership and authority to the lowest levels of the organization; an approach supported by research as improving student achievement.

Accountability

Most boards have placed a strong focus on this topic; some would argue too much. Indeed, often multiple board standards seem to focus primarily on holding the school personnel accountable for increasing test scores. The language in this element differs from that model in several ways. First, the board's focus is on student "learning," not test scores. Second, accountability is placed squarely upon the board itself as well as school personnel for student learning. Third, accountability is defined by the assurance of alignment of vision, policy, resources, staffing, curriculum, and professional development with improved student learning; not just the monitoring of test scores from year to year. Finally, the element reminds the board of the importance of support and celebration of success of personnel. This marks a contrast with a culture of high-stakes accountability where the message is that faculty performance is never good enough.

Using Data for Continuous Improvement

The use of data for decision making has become a major topic for school boards and school personnel alike. Most boards focus on this standard, emphasizing the need to use data to monitor student achievement. Of course, this primarily means monitoring test scores. The element language provides the push for setting high expectations, but also makes clear that some activities within the organization need to be maintained. Often, continuous improvement standards have prompted boards to expect frequent and pervasive change while not supporting system improvement over system replacement.

The element language is explicit in its requirement that the school board use multiple data sources in multiple formats. It is currently not uncommon for boards that have so-called use of data goals to focus only on test scores from a single test—test scores that represent large groups of students that are not individually analyzed or tracked by cohort. Current systems that track the performance of individual students over time often produce very different realities of where intervention is needed and what type of intervention is necessary. An example of how multiple data from multiple sources can provide solutions to student achievement issues is illustrated in figure 6.2. As shown, additional information could lead to very different or additional conclusions and solutions that can be more successful in helping student improve their learning. In the example, it is important that all teachers understand and practice culturally sensitive teaching methods; however, this may not be the cause of lower scores and certainly does not address lower scores among all students. The additional data would not only support the board in implementing solutions to enhance cultural sensitivity, but would also prompt them to support other solutions to address the concerns.

Cultural Responsiveness

This element is simply missing from most school board standards of excellence. The element provides context by focusing on diversity within each community. Indeed, within some school districts generational, political, or economic diversity may influence board effectiveness and their ability to hear the voices of all stakeholders in addition to the more prominent focus on racial, ethnic, and gender diversity. The point here is that all forms of diverse thought and ideology are

Figure 6.2 Use of multiple source data in solving student achievement issues

Test data	Multiple source data
Test score disaggregation shows that African American males are scoring well below White students	Individual student assessment indicates that some African American male students are performing well and some poorly. In addition, some White students are performing poorly as well. Information regarding the home life of students indicates that students of poverty, students of highly mobile families, and students with parents with evening work shifts perform worse.
Possible solutions?	*Additional solutions?*
#1. Provide all teachers with professional development training on better understanding and celebrating diverse culture.	#1: Interview each student, regardless of race, and determine who is struggling and why. Design individual learning improvement plans for each student based on individual need.
#2. Require all teachers to teach using culturally sensitive instructional methods.	#2: Provide or require a full support program for students before and after school including meals, activities, and individualized instructional stations for students who are struggling.

critical to the board's success. As with many of the Elements of Success standards, individual tools have been developed to assist boards in better understanding the standard and applying it to their own circumstances. Figure 6.3 provides a list of questions that helps school boards develop an *equity lens* to use in making decisions and better implementing equitable practices and policies.[1] The equity lens provides a common vocabulary and protocol for resource allocation and evaluating educational investment decisions.

Climate

This standard is often included in lists of board effectiveness but is generally focused on school safety issues and satisfaction surveys administered to the community and staff. The element points to a much broader conception of climate that some might better understand as "culture." Effective boards must monitor measures of organizational culture, like a belief that "all students can learn," or that

Figure 6.3   Questions for use by a school board in implementing an equity lens

Objective: By utilizing an equity lens, and the guiding questions below, the school board aims to encourage and assess the board's focus on creating a district with cultural responsiveness.

The following questions will be considered for evaluating strategic policy decisions and how these decisions are culturally responsive:

1. Who are the racial/ethnic and underserved groups affected? What is the potential impact of the resource allocation or the strategic policy decisions to these groups?

2. Does the decision being made ignore or worsen existing disparities or produce other unintended consequences? What is the impact on eliminating the opportunity gap?

3. How does the policy decision or resource allocation advance the goal for 40 percent of all students graduating from four year colleges, 40 percent graduating with two-year degrees, and 20 percent completing their education with a high school diploma (the 40/40/20 goal)?

4. What are the barriers to more equitable outcomes (e.g., mandated, political, emotional, financial, programmatic, or managerial)?

5. How have you intentionally involved stakeholders who are also members of the communities affected by the strategic policy decision or resource allocation?

6. How will you modify or enhance your strategies to ensure each learner and communities' individual and cultural needs are met?

7. How are you collecting data on racial/ethnic, native language, impoverished, or other underserved student groups?

8. What is your commitment to P-20 professional learning for equity? What resources are you allocating for training in cultural responsive instruction?

"all opinions (positive and negative) are valued and heard," or that "diverse culture is understood and valued because it makes us more successful." There are organizational monitoring surveys[2] that measure variables of culture that go far beyond the typical climate survey used in most districts. This element's language would prompt a much deeper assessment of organizational health by the school board.

Learning Organizations and Systems Thinking

Most boards include the need for board members to engage in professional development training. These two elements take the concept to a deeper level by placing a goal before the school board to ensure that the entire school organization be provided professional development that empowers staff and nurtures leadership capabilities across the system. In addition, the elements use terms like the importance of "reflection," "discovery," and "self-renewal" to describe effective professional development. This becomes critical because most professional development has a focus on compliance mandates like inculcating among all faculty a mandated new curriculum, assessment, or evaluation program rather than offering individualized professional development. In addition, the concepts of "learning organization" and "systems thinking" address how the organization as a whole is improving, not just the delivery of new knowledge to individual teachers or leaders. This involves the consideration of how each individual is interacting with each other and how that supports or reduces improvement efforts. Therefore, the focus of this element is not only new knowledge but how that new knowledge aligns and fits into existing systems.

Innovation and Creativity

This element is generally absent from board standards. Often standards of accountability and use of data produce board actions that run counter to supporting innovation, creativity, and experimentation among faculty. This element recognizes that innovation and creativity are assets to the process of development and change, leading to new types of thinking and better ways of meeting student needs. Innovation and creativity can flourish when boards align vision throughout the organization, engage in collaborative partnerships, and encourage dialogue, new ideas, and differing perspectives.

SUPPORTING FEATURES OF ELEMENTS OF SUCCESS
Indicators

The Elements of Success tool includes indicators for each element. Indicators express what we expect to see if this element is actually successfully implemented and in place in a district. Indicators can also provide a to-do list of concrete actions a board puts in place in order to move forward on that element. Let's take a look at Vision Directed Planning as an example (see figure 6.4). A board may well have put in place a vision and mission statement, and a long-range plan that involves community input. Check, right? But wait a minute, this element also talks about aligning the budget and resources to the vision and goals. For many boards and districts, this is a unique concept. Oh yes, we build a budget that includes funding the things we talk about in our goals, but do we really ALIGN it? When the question "What do we cut?" comes up, what do we use to decide what gets cut? Is the first thing we use to analyze the situation our goals and strategic plan? For many districts, whether it is cutting or adding, changes to the budget are more of a political process than an analytical one of what best moves our goals forward. To truly be a Vision-Directed Planning district, all decisions, including (if not most importantly) budget decisions, must be made through the lens of the district's vision and goals.

Adaptive elements such as Innovation and Creativity typically require more time and process to put in place, but again, the indicators can be used by the board

Figure 6.4 Indicators for the Elements of Success

ELEMENT #1 Vision-Directed Planning. Boards engage communities and staff in the development of a shared vision of student learning. The vision is the foundation of the mission and goals that direct board policy making, planning, resource allocation, and activities.

Indicators for this element are:

1. The board collaborates with the community to articulate core values and beliefs for the district.

2. Board members can clearly articulate the vision and goals of the district.

3. The board has developed a long-range plan for improving student learning.

4. The board regularly monitors the progress of goals to improve student learning.

5. The board adopts a budget and appropriates resources aligned to the vision and goals.

6. The board establishes a culture of high expectations for all students.

---

to assess where the board and district are to start, and how to move forward. For example, the first indicator for Innovation and Creativity is "Board members create time and opportunity for their own creative thinking." The board can discuss what this means to them and the administration, and how to implement creative thinking. This can occur within current board agendas, a work session or other more informal meeting, or through reading books that stimulate creative discussions. Most of these indicators drive more in-depth conversations regarding what success will look like, as well as how to get there.

Expert Comments

Unlike most other standards, the Elements of Success document provides research citations supporting not only the elements but also each of the indicators. In addition to the indicators provided to better define each element (see the example in figure 6.4), the document provides expert commentary that further describes effective board action. For example, under Element #1, Vision-Directed Planning, expert comments include the following examples, each linked to supporting documentation:

> What separates a learning community from an ordinary school is its collective commitment to guiding principles that articulate what the people in the school believe and what they seek to create. Furthermore, these guiding principles are not just articulated by those in positions of leadership; even more important, they are embedded in the hearts and minds of people throughout the school.[3]
>
> . . .
>
> Create organizational clarity. Organizational clarity is not merely about choosing the right words to describe an organization's mission, strategy, or values; it is about agreeing on the fundamental concepts that drive it. An organization that has achieved clarity has a sense of unity around everything it does. It aligns resources, especially the human ones, around common concepts, values, definitions, goals, and strategies.[4]

This additional treasure trove of supporting expert commentary provide school board members with the ability to fully understand the meaning and intent of effectiveness standards. This is critical in that often standards are not fully understood or are misinterpreted—at times producing board values, beliefs, and decisions that run counter to the "best practices" they hope to support. Often this is done unwittingly by boards who don't fully grasp the meaning of research on effective schools. The creation of a vision focused on the belief that all students can learn is a good example of this confusion. Often, boards adopt this standard but make decisions that attempt to *mandate* a culture of high expectation rather than working to *transform* the school culture as addressed in the expert commentary noted above. The Elements of Success support the notion that board members are fully capable of understanding these distinctions if given adequate opportunity to discuss and collaboratively understand the shared standards they hope to support together.

Using the Elements of Success

As mentioned previously, the Elements of Success can be used by school boards as a list of board standards or goals. The elements can then be easily used as an annual board assessment that measures not only its own effectiveness, but the success of the school district in enacting organizational goals and practices that are linked to higher and more equitable student achievement. In addition, the elements can be used periodically by an external evaluator to measure board effectiveness. The Elements of Success are each supported by substantial research on effective boards and support a Balanced Governance approach where board members are informed and knowledgeable in their oversight of not only surface outcomes (e.g., test scores) but deep and lasting organizational change like innovation, systems health, or cultural responsiveness—elements that allow a school board to leave a legacy of sustainable improvement in its district.

7

Assessing Individual Board Members

A Self-Assessment for Improved Board Performance

Thomas L. Alsbury

The effective performance of the school board to support student learning is a topic that is critical and timely. Consequently, researchers and practitioners in school board governance are turning their attention to discovering and applying ways to improve the effectiveness of elected school boards through a variety of approaches.

EXISTING BOARD TRAINING

It is critical that school boards engage in relevant and effective training. In the training and development of school boards, it is important that all board members and the superintendent engage in training as a team. In addition, the topics covered in school board development make a real difference. In the past, school board training tended to consist of practical and important topics such as understanding the budget, following legal requirements (e.g., open public meeting laws), and how to run an efficient board meeting. Recently, training for school boards has begun to focus more on understanding how to support instructional improvement and data-driven decision making.

Another important way to improve the performance of school boards is the development of various protocols and guides practiced by the board as a whole. These include the adoption of school board standards, rules for board meeting conduct, the development of strategic goals, and group agreements on processes for decision making when reviewing and adopting policy or resolving problems. Again, all of these elements are critical to the smooth operation of the school board.

However, missing from the conversation regarding the board's performance has been a focus on the characteristics needed by each board member that most support the effective performance of the board as a whole. Individual board member characteristics are important to address, because overall board dysfunction can result from even a single board member's beliefs, values, and behavior.

Indeed, a school board could establish an excellent strategic plan and engage in efficient school board meeting procedures but still fall into a contentious and dysfunctional pattern because of how individual board members behave. Thankfully, research findings on school board effectiveness apply not just to the board as a whole, but to individual board member characteristics and beliefs. More specifically, studies have identified individual board member characteristics found in *stable*, high performing school boards.

THE IMPORTANCE OF STABILITY

One might wonder why *stabilizing* a school board is necessary or even desirable. First, it is important to describe clearly what a stable board means. For example, a stable board could refer to a board with very little turnover. However, in this chapter, the term *stable* refers to a school board that is operating effectively, efficiently, and collaboratively. Stability does not necessarily refer to the amount of turnover, but instead what we will call *stabilizing factors* present on the board. These include:

- Stability of board operations
- Stability of board working relationships
- Stability of board expectations for district personnel
- Stability of board goals for student improvement

While an overall increase in board member turnover can cause a decline in these stabilizing factors, turnover alone does not necessarily create less stability. In fact, research clearly shows the importance of distinguishing between what we call stabilizing (politically motivated) turnover and destabilizing (apolitically motivated turnover).[1] *Stabilizing turnover* is school board turnover that does not lead to a dramatic change in the goals and direction, the smooth operation, or the working relationship of the board and superintendent. Indeed, stabilizing turnover is often a result of board members leaving the board, or choosing not to run again, due to a board member

- moving out of the community or the district representing their seat;
- suffering a personal illness or illness of a family member;
- experiencing work or personal obligations that no longer allow the time needed to serve; or
- feeling they have served long enough and that it is time to give someone else a turn.

On the other hand, *destabilizing turnover* is characterized by a board member

- losing a board election;
- resigning from the board or refusing to run due to pressure from the public;
- leaving or choosing not to run due to persistent conflict with other board members or the superintendent; or
- leaving or choosing not to run due to a disagreement with the direction of the majority of the board, superintendent, and/or the public.

The dissatisfaction of the public is believed to be the most significant factor leading to destabilizing turnover of school board members. A key governance theory known as the Dissatisfaction Theory of American Democracy supports this idea.[2] The theory accurately describes what happens when school boards experience increased levels of destabilizing school board turnover. As shown in figure 7.1, which represents an application of the Dissatisfaction Theory of American Democracy, destabilizing school board behavior leads to destabilizing school board turnover.

One characteristic of destabilizing board turnover is that incoming board members typically run on, and desire to implement, an agenda to change the policies, procedures, and/or personnel of the school district. In this case, an incoming board member, who is joining the board as a result of destabilizing election defeat

Figure 7.1   Results of destabilizing school board turnover

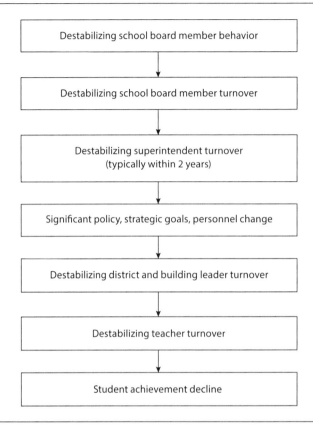

or pressured resignation, may identify particular teachers or leaders they are tar-geting to replace. Frequently, the superintendent is such a target.[3]

In fact, studies consistently show that destabilizing school board member be-haviors lead to destabilizing school board turnover, which leads to destabilizing superintendent turnover.[4] As shown in figure 7.1, destabilizing superintendent turnover frequently leads to hiring a new superintendent who brings a different agenda to the district—generally reflective of the new board members' interests and often substantially different from those of the outgoing superintendent. This often leads to changes in policy, procedures, and a variety of work conditions, which changes the district culture. While these changes may be considered posi-tive, if they occur too frequently they result in increased turnover of key school leaders. This is because the superintendent and district leaders supervise and evaluate school leaders based upon established goals, current school culture, and past organizational practice.

Frequent destabilizing turnover in school board leadership results in a loss of organizational memory and a lack of experience on the board to guide new board members. Destabilizing turnover in superintendent leadership often has a cascading effect, leading to a decline in staff morale, an increased feeling of insecurity among staff, a discontinuity in district/school goals and purpose, declining community confidence, and an increased culture of protectionism and compliance. The result of the introduction of uncertainty and constant change in district goals and purpose prompts the best and brightest of school leaders and teachers to seek employment elsewhere, where goals and expectations are clear and consistent. Finally, when capable school leaders and teachers leave the district, student learning suffers.

Not All Board Turnover Is Bad

Certainly, change can sometimes improve a board; however, frequent turnover and contentious relations among board members are counterproductive. It is important to reiterate that stabilizing board turnover does not typically lead to the sequence of events described in figure 7.1. This is because with stabilizing turnover, incoming board members tend to support the goals and practices of outgoing incumbents and therefore tend not to push for dramatic changes in policy or the replacement of school personnel. As a result, stabilizing board turnover can be benign, because it does not lead to the type of destabilizing change connected with lower student achievement.[5]

The Need for Individualized Characteristics

So far, we have established that distinguishing between destabilizing and stabilizing board turnover is important. We've determined that destabilizing school board member beliefs and behavior lead to increased destabilizing board turnover, increased destabilizing superintendent turnover, and lower student performance. Therefore, it is critical to identify and avoid individual school board member beliefs and behaviors that cause the destabilizing turnover. Even more important is the need to understand and promote stabilizing school board member characteristics.

STABILIZING SCHOOL BOARD MEMBER CHARACTERISTICS

Research on school board effectiveness is frequently applied to the characteristics of the board as a whole group. However, the same findings can provide a guide to the most stabilizing (and therefore effective) *individual* beliefs and behaviors among school board members. Figure 7.2 lists stabilizing board member characteristics along with a brief description of each. Individuals can use the stabilizing school board characteristics as a tool for self-assessment and reflection.

An effective use of the stabilizing board member characteristics listed in figure 7.2 is as a self-assessment tool for personal reflection and improvement for individual board members. While the comments and the will of the voting public critique the board as a whole during election time, there is little opportunity for individual self-assessment. Board members already may receive individual criticism from some members of the public. Because of this, board members would be understandably reluctant to open themselves up for further personal criticism. Even if they do remain open to community critique, the public is generally not aware of the most critical and effective criteria of good board performance. The list of stabilizing board member characteristics provides a personal, private, and informed method for self-improvement that connects with student achievement gains.

Each of the ten stabilizing board member characteristics requires a certain level of explanation and understanding before it can be fully applied to the uses noted above. Often the stabilizing topic will be familiar to the reader, but the topic may be more complicated in its application. This does not create a problem in using the tool—it simply means that further explanation on how to understand and apply the tool to improve board performance is necessary. While it is beyond the scope of this chapter to cover all ten stabilizing characteristics, two are explained here to illustrate their subtle meaning and how they might be applied in real life scenarios.

Role Boundaries

The characteristic of role boundaries refers to the need for a board member to understand and then practice the balance between *oversight* and *micromanagement*. This characteristic reflects both belief and behavior. This particular stabilizing belief will be familiar to most board members, because it is a common concept

Figure 7.2 Stabilizing characteristics for individual school board members

Board member characteristic	Brief description	Stabilizing characteristic
1. Role boundaries	Understands the difference between the role of **oversight** and **micromanagement**.	**Oversight** with knowledgeable critique and advocacy.
2. Role orientation	A **trustee** speaks for general interests and assumes a personal mandate due to their election, valuing unanimity on board decisions. A **delegate** attempts to speak for special interests, comfortable with open debate and split votes to maintain a platform for diverse and competing interests.	**Trustee** with the ability to shift to delegate in times of emerging conflict, community dissatisfaction, or change
3. Advocacy focus	A **position-driven focus** is often polarizing and identifies "friends" and "enemies." An **interest-driven focus** seeks to satisfy multiple and diverse needs and avoids the narrow demands of special interests.	**Interest-driven**
4. Student concern focus	Supports a **broad** focus on student concerns. A stated responsibility to insure all students are afforded social justice. Avoids **targeted** focus justice for single categories of students or needs.	**Broad focus** of social justice for all students
5. Solution focus	Understands that the local school district, and each school, has **unique and shifting needs**, often requiring **nonstandard solutions**.	Recognizes **contextual need** Supports **creative, nonstandard solutions**
6. Exercise of influence and visibility	Understands that board members possess **no individual authority.** Power rests in the board as a group only.	School board **team influence** and **supportive visibility**
7. Use of voice*	Does the board member use his or her voice to **tell and sell** their position or do they seek to listen, understand interests, and discover **resolution and reconciliation?**	Uses voice to **listen, resolve, and reconcile**
8. Use of power*	**Power Over** is using your position to get your own way through threat or reward. **Power With** is using your position to ensure all voices are heard and collaborative solutions are guaranteed.	**Power With**
9. Decision-making style*	Decision making can be done **individually** and quickly or can be done **collaboratively** with and through others.	**Collaborative**
10. Motivation for service*	Board members can serve for **personal** or for **altruistic** reasons.	**Altruistic service**

*For more on these characteristics, see Meredith Mountford, "Historical and Current Tensions Among Board-Superintendent Teams: Symptoms or Causes?" in *The Future of School Board Governance: Relevancy and Revelation*, ed. Thomas L. Alsbury (Lanham, MD: Rowman & Littlefield, 2008), 81–114.

covered in most basic board training. However, despite its commonness, it is highly possible to miss the subtleties of this characteristic.

In general, most board members have heard that their role is one of oversight and not management. However, as always, the devil is in the details. For example, some school board training recommends that board members should serve their oversight role by engaging in only two activities—hiring the superintendent and approving policy. In fact, some board governance models indicate that board members should only set measureable outcome goals in policy, sometimes resulting in tracking test scores exclusively. The board may then be instructed to inquire only about whether the overall test average for an entire grade was reached or not. A board member that would like to inquire *how* the test score was to be raised may be accused of micromanaging. In many governance models, the board is restricted to the inquiry and oversight of test outcomes only and discouraged from inquiring about or understanding programs or processes.

However, as discussed in the introduction to this book, research and practicing board members have come to the same conclusion: *oversight* requires knowledgeable critique and advocacy. What this means is that it is not reasonable to suggest that the board be restricted from learning about some of the processes. For example, board members on highly effective boards tend to seek answers to questions such as the following when overseeing progress on math scores:

1. What are the math score trends for cohorts? Comparing score changes between different classes of students is not an indicator of learning improvement because classes of students can perform very differently.
2. What are the cohort score trends if disaggregated by ethnicity, language, gender, mobility of the parent(s), poverty, etc.? While federal reform policies (e.g., No Child Left Behind) require some of these disaggregated scores, the individual community context, need, and performance may call for disaggregating additional groups of students' scores.
3. What do student-learning trends look like if tracked by individual student? There can be some students doing poorly within an overall high performing group. Conversely, there may be a small group of excellent performers in an overall low performing group. Board members should ask how students are being assisted if they don't follow the performance of their identified

group—either by overperforming or underperforming in comparison. This can also help avoid throwing out entire programs when focused revision to an existing program may be warranted. This also prevents applying a blanket solution to a specific need.

4. How does performance compare from one school to the next within the district? This may reveal trends in high performance to study and replicate. Likewise, some schools may need special assistance and additional resources.

5. What specific area of math is problematic? Students might be doing well in computation but not in problem solving. If this was evident, board members could make more informed decisions regarding program adoption to ensure that problem areas are addressed with focused solutions and not answered with simply replacing the entire curriculum.

6. In the case of a recommended new instructional program, what in the new program specifically addresses the needs our students have? Once again, rather than a general sales job that sings the praises of the newest flavor-of-the-month, solutions should be matched to specific needs. Often the best solution is a locally developed program over a nationally applied one-size-fits-all.

7. Is the new program research-based? If so, please provide a summary of the research findings. It has become popular to claim that all programs are research-based. In reality, often the research is mixed on the effectiveness of programs. Often, the only research performed on the product is by the seller. In one recent example of a "best practice" math program, a quick check on the company website revealed that results were mixed and inconclusive for the program. It was also clear what the program would and would not improve within math learning.

The list could go on. The point here is that board members asking these questions are engaged not in micromanagement, but in what I call *informed oversight*. In other words, the board member is able to understand what the problems are in a general way, and expects an explanation of how the new program or approach will address specific needs. This allows board members to not only make an informed decision on program adoption, but also converse intelligently with the public to support the interventions used by the district.

Notice that in the questions above, the board members are not telling the administration or staff which program to choose or how to implement it. The board member also does not criticize or recommend how the superintendent should resolve a need that does not appear to be met. Therefore, this board, when practicing informed oversight, is not crossing a line into micromanaging.

Some might suggest that the description of the balance between micromanagement and oversight, as presented above, may seem too challenging for board members. However, there is no evidence to support this concern. First, board members are highly educated, with nearly 70 percent holding college degrees. Further, this type of informed oversight is distinctive among highly effective boards. In fact, uninformed school board members tend to be viewed as *rubber-stampers* and cheerleaders or critics by many community members. This leads to a lack of trust and confidence on the part of the public. When board members cannot address school issues in a direct and knowledgeable manner, they are left to govern through political leveraging, rather than informed decision making based on what is best for students. Uninformed oversight encourages board members and the public to engage in questioning and criticizing school operations, management, and personnel. Thus, an uninformed board more often becomes a micromanaging board. Ironically, the effort to keep the board out of the business of the school administrator through the practice of uninformed oversight can create a knowledge vacuum that tends to be filled with second-guessing management.

Role Orientation: Trustee Versus Delegate

Another individual stabilizing board member characteristic involves the appropriate orientation that a board member should have as he or she engages in balanced, informed oversight. While a number of different roles have been defined for board members, board orientation is less commonly discussed. A Balanced Governance approach would include careful consideration of the *trustee* versus *delegate* orientation.[6]

Describing the Orientations.   School board members do not commonly know what is meant by the terms *trustee* and *delegate*. These role orientations can be viewed as forming a continuum, with most board members positioned somewhere between the two extremes. However, most board members generally favor one end or the other, believing that is their appropriate function as a board member. As I'll show below, most effective board members understand that they should act sometimes in the trustee orientation and sometimes in the delegate orientation. This represents another example of the importance of taking a Balanced Governance approach.

Board members who favor the trustee end of the continuum

- tend to view themselves as representing the general interests of the community;
- believe that the community vote placed a trust with them to act in the school's best interests;
- do not seek out or vote based on the demands of special interests of particular individuals or groups;
- do not vote on their own beliefs or interests but on what they believe is best for the whole;
- do not favor open debate of diverse viewpoints in school board meetings;
- tend to restrict their actions to policy approval and uninformed oversight; and
- prefer unanimous votes on board decisions.

Members with a trustee orientation prefer that the board present a united front. They believe that unity is preferable to special interests. They do not seek out frequent input from the community, as diverse and often opposing viewpoints tend to disrupt the board's goal continuity.

The other end of the continuum is the *delegate* orientation. Board members who favor this orientation

- tend to view themselves as representing their own interests;
- believe that the community vote placed them as a representative to speak for special interest groups that got them elected;
- vote based on the demands of special interests of particular individuals or groups;
- seek continuous conversation with diverse and opposing viewpoints;
- do not restrict their actions to approving outcome-based policy but seek process information;

- favor open debate of diverse viewpoints in school board meetings; and
- encourage split votes on board decisions.

Members with a delegate orientation view themselves as representative spokespersons or advocates for their own personal interests or for special interest groups. Their view of a transparent, democratic approach to board service is to advocate for continual open communication with a broad and often diverse constituency. They tend to act independently and avoid unanimity, believing that unanimous votes reflect a rubber-stamp board approach that is the sign of poor board governance. They view their role as encouraging all voices to be heard and all viewpoints debated openly, with their personal goal to argue for and win acceptance of their own preferred viewpoint. Members with this orientation also believe that it is necessary to inquire about management and operations processes in order to engage in proper and thorough oversight of the district.

Growing Preference for the Delegate Orientation.   Many factors influence a board member's decision on whether to adopt a trustee or delegate orientation. A historical overview indicates that the delegate orientation is becoming more and more prevalent. It is believed that this is the result of a dramatic increase in the cultural diversity within communities, leading to the rise of special interest groups competing with each other for opposing needs and wants. In addition, the decline in the confidence and trust of public officials has led to the interest in board members inquiring into management and operations rather than the less political role of approving policy and deferring to the wisdom of the superintendent.

The delegate orientation appears on the surface to be more democratic in its encouragement of open debate of multiple viewpoints. The delegate approach plays into an American notion of personal independence and voice being of number one importance. In addition, the community, when asked to choose between delegate and trustee orientations, selects the delegate orientation more often.

Delegate Orientation Is Usually Destabilizing.   Despite the immediate popularity of the delegate orientation with the public and its growing use by board members, delegate orientation is destabilizing.[7] In fact, using the extreme of delegate orientation results in confrontations between board members and the public in school board meetings. The public's response to viewing the delegate orientation in action, despite what they might say they prefer, is negative. While the idea of engaging in open debates between multiple and opposing special interests seems democratic, the public responds by reporting a loss of confidence in the board's leadership when this is practiced. The public views the board as being in conflict, lacking strong leadership and direction, and describes the board as dysfunctional. Sometimes school boards practicing this approach are described as a three-ring circus. In the end, destabilizing board member behavior and turnover result from board members practicing an extreme form of delegate orientation.

Trustee Orientation Is Usually Stable.   Board members usually learn through experience that the most stable and supported approach to their service on the board is a trustee orientation. Board members understand that while they may keep up-to-date with various constituents and special interests, it is best to come to consensus with fellow board members and ultimately show a united front with mostly unanimous votes. The public generally seems more satisfied with this approach, and board member seats are more stable with less destabilizing board and superintendent turnover.

Balanced Governance Orientation Is Best.   It may appear from the discussion above that board members should always use a trustee orientation. However, while this is generally better, the most effective boards balance their use of trustee and delegate orientations. Generally, the trustee behavior is stabilizing. Nonetheless, it can tend to be insulating, because in order to keep a united front to the public, diverse interests and voices can seem to be ignored as boards look within their team to maintain collaboration and a team culture. This approach works well in school district environments that are relatively stable and satisfied with the board's performance.

However, communities can change in the balance of their interests. For example, a community's socioeconomic status can change due to migration. A previously rural community may change when an expanding city turns them into a suburb. Events like crime or racial discord can change a community's needs and desires. Boards operating with the trustee orientation can easily miss noticing the critical nature of community changes. If a board ignores these changes, community dissatisfaction can grow quickly, leading to destabilizing turnover on the board.

Perceptive board members watch for and monitor cultural, economic, and social changes and understand the importance of shifting from a trustee to a delegate orientation in times of emerging conflict, community dissatisfaction, or other change. The board in essence looks outside itself to show empathy and interest, re-identify community needs, and adjust policy to match those needs. When the community is satisfied with the adjustment, the board can return to the trustee orientation.

ADDITIONAL USES OF STABILIZING CHARACTERISTICS

We've discussed how the stabilizing characteristics described in figure 7.2 can improve collegiality and teamwork on the school board, which in turn can lead to improved board performance and student achievement. However, the list can also be used to assist in improving the performance of individual board members and boards as a whole in at least three additional ways.

Board Candidates

Understanding stabilizing board member characteristics is instructive not only for established boards but also as a guide for those considering running for a seat. Candidates could use the list to develop a plan for campaigning as well as providing a tool for personal reflection and critique. Supporters and advisors could use the list to give guidance to a candidate.

Often the things that candidates use to win election to the school board can actually harm their ability to function on the board once elected. For example, a candidate might run for the board with a single issue to improve the performance of a particular group of students. Politically, it is likely that board candidates could be pressured to run on single and focused agendas by groups with special interests. However, an important reality for a school board member is that they do not hold any power individually. School boards only operate as a team. In fact, research indicates that the ability for board members to function as a board team is the best predictor of the effectiveness of a school board.[8]

The most successful board candidate not only must win the board seat but also do so in a way that allows him or her to work effectively with fellow board members as a team. Focusing on single issues can polarize and alienate a school board member from the board. This can lead to conflict, open debate, and split votes, which raise concerns by the public about the ability of a board to be effective. The result is that voters remove incumbent board members with a single-issue focus at a much higher rate.

When this occurs, single-issue board members do not actually get anything accomplished for their special interest. Even when they are not defeated, conflict among the board often delays improvements for their special interest. One of the stabilizing characteristics listed in figure 7.2 addresses this situation. Characteristic 3, advocacy focus, recommends that board members replace standing on *position* with standing on *interest*. In our current discussion, the candidate could campaign on meeting the needs of all underperforming students by redirecting resources to students needing assistance. This approach moves the candidate away from standing on an exclusive and polarizing position that may later cause disharmony on the school board. It puts the board member where he or she should be in terms of ability to effect change through the board as a whole rather than through individual advocacy or activism.

Voter Education

Another way the list of stabilizing board member characteristics can be used is as a voter's guide to help the public determine how best to select incoming board members. Figure 7.2 provides voters with a list of predictors of how stabilizing and effective each candidate may be on the existing board. For example, a board candidate might express, during the campaign, that he or she would spend time in schools to ensure that teachers and leaders were doing their job. According to research[9]—and reflected in the stabilizing board member characteristics—this tactic would likely not lead to school improvement; in fact, quite the opposite. Because the public is responsible for electing their school board, it is imperative that they be educated on which characteristics in a board member tend to lead to improved student performance.

External Evaluation

Finally, an external evaluator could use the list of stabilizing beliefs and behaviors to measure observed board behaviors and interactions. The items in figure 7.2 could be used as a template to review board members as they perform their duties. An external evaluator might observe members at board meetings, work sessions, and even at public events. An external evaluator could note the board members' conversations, questions, and behaviors, and compare those against the stabilizing board member characteristics. In this way, board members could be provided with an individualized and personal assessment of their performance. In addition, the entire board could receive an overall board profile with individual results recorded, without identifying individuals. The profile would provide a helpful set of assessment data that the board could use to discuss how to improve their overall performance as well as guide them in creating operating protocols to improve their work.

UNDERSTANDING AND USING THE STABILIZING CHARACTERISTICS

Unpacking two of the stabilizing board characteristics from figure 7.2 demonstrates how they relate to real-life situations and emphasizes the need to understand the subtleties of all ten characteristics. The examples show that some characteristics may be unfamiliar to current board members (e.g., trustee vs. delegate orientation). Other, more familiar characteristics (e.g., oversight vs. micromanagement) still require further understanding and guidance on how to apply them.

Together, the ten stabilizing board member characteristics provide a comprehensive tool for individual board member self-assessment and reflection and for educating the public on the appropriate roles for board members that lead to improved student performance. The tool advocates for the balanced use of each of the characteristics and could be a valuable addition to board assessment for school boards that seek to improve their effectiveness and their district's performance.

8

Superintendent Evaluation

An Opportunity to Strengthen Board Practice

Phil Gore and Larry Nyland

INTRODUCTION

Evaluation of the superintendent can be challenging for school boards and superintendents alike. It can also be an excellent opportunity for district improvement. An effective evaluation highlights a strong board-superintendent relationship, which is critical for student success. When a board and superintendent work together on superintendent evaluation, both become stronger. Superintendent evaluation can align the board's policy role with the superintendent's administrative role. This chapter begins with a consideration of the opportunities superintendent evaluation offers for improving school governance. In the second half, we offer practical suggestions from research, promising practices, and our unique experiences as a school board member and superintendent.

Typically, superintendents serve at the will of the board. One purpose of evaluation is to help decide whether to keep the superintendent or justify a raise. A simple thumbs-up or thumbs-down might suffice on keeping the superintendent. Individual board members likely know before the formal evaluation whether they want to keep their superintendent. The same might be true for whether to give the superintendent a raise.

A second, arguably more important purpose for superintendent evaluation is improving student learning. Some studies indicate that evaluating a superintendent on student learning goals may relate more with improving student achievement than any other action of a board. Setting student learning goals for the superintendent and communicating those to the community has been positively associated with improved achievement.[1] Boards and superintendents working together to define measurable goals for student learning is a promising practice.

A third purpose for evaluation is to improve leadership skills of superintendents. We know more about effective leadership today than ever before. Research-based superintendent frameworks carefully describe differing levels of performance. Frameworks provide a clear pathway to growth—from unsatisfactory to distinguished—and give both the board and superintendent clear descriptions of improved leadership. One example of an effective evaluation framework is the Washington Association of School Administrators/Washington State School Directors Association Superintendent Framework, an excerpt from which is shown in figure 8.1.

Promising practices in this superintendent framework include: four tiers of performance with no middle ground or neutral option, a clear progression across the tiers, and concrete examples of observable performance. The top tier, distinguished, is characterized by systemwide impact and leadership recognized by peers.

SCHOOL BOARD MEMBERS

Board Members As Evaluators

School board members are more educated and more likely to come from highly valued professions than is the average citizen. They tend to be vested in their communities and serve on numerous other boards and committees. Most of them have previous experience in evaluating employees, individually and as part of a team. Many board members may be well qualified for the task of performing superintendent evaluation.

Nonetheless, the role of a superintendent is complex and unique. Superintendents are also well-educated, experienced, dedicated, and trusted public servants.

Figure 8.1 Excerpt from Washington State Superintendent leadership framework

STANDARD 2—Instructional Leadership: The superintendent is an educational leader who improves learning and achievement for each student by advocating, nurturing, and sustaining a district culture conducive to student learning and staff professional growth.

STRAND 1—Putting student learning at the center. The superintendent . . .

Themes	Unsatisfactory	Basic	Proficient	Distinguished
A. advocates for student learning as the district's highest priority	does not communicate that student learning is central to the district's mission	communicates to all stakeholders that student learning is central to the district's mission	consistently emphasizes student learning is central to the district mission by actively engaging stakeholders in collaborative discussion of ways to improve learning	motivates stakeholders to seek continuous improvement and innovation in student learning to achieve the district's mission
B. promotes the systematic improvement of curriculum, instruction, and assessment	takes few steps to analyze district curriculum, instruction, and assessment to improve student learning	engages staff in regular analysis of district curriculum, instruction, and assessment	assures that decisions on curriculum, instruction, and assessment are guided by regular analysis based on objective data	develops or sustains a comprehensive system for the review, analysis and modification of curriculum, instruction, and assessment based on key learning indicators
C. assures that district policies, practices, and resources support student learning	does not align district policies, practices, and resources to support student learning	assures that existing district policies, practices, and resources are aligned to support student learning	uses data to seek improvements in district policies, practices, and resources to better support student learning	motivates principals and other administrators, teachers, and other members of the school community to seek improvement in district policies, practices, and resources to support student learning
D. promotes values, beliefs and behaviors that create an organizational culture devoted to student learning	does not address the values, beliefs, behaviors, and organizational practices that support a school culture focused on student learning	recognizes and celebrates individual and collective efforts that reinforce the culture to improve student learning	creates or sustains a culture that leads members of the school community to openly acknowledge and collaboratively address problems in student learning	creates or sustains a sense of collective mission and efficacy in the improvement of student learning
E. gives a high priority to reducing achievement gaps	disregards or downplays the significance of achievement gaps	focuses attention on the need to maintain high expectations for each student and close achievement gaps	assures that improvement efforts include data-based strategies to analyze and address barriers to student learning and setting specific targets for closing achievement gaps	creates districtwide commitment to understanding and addressing achievement gaps, and demonstrates sustained progress in improving learning

continued

Figure 8.1 *continued*

STANDARD 6—Socio-Political Context: The superintendent is an educational leader who improves learning and achievement for each student by understanding, responding to, and influencing the political, social, economic, legal, and cultural context.

STRAND 2—Works effectively with the school district's Board of Directors. The superintendent . . .

Themes	Unsatisfactory	Basic	Proficient	Distinguished
A. respects and advocates mutual understanding of the roles and responsibilities of superintendents and board	does not articulate or adhere to the roles and responsibilities of the board and superintendent	articulates and adheres to the roles and responsibilities of the superintendent and board	collaborates with board to review and refine guidelines for effective board and superintendent roles and responsibilities	models candid but respectful discussion of board and superintendent roles and responsibilities, including areas of friction or misunderstanding in the board-superintendent relationship
B. honors board policy	does not follow board policy	follows board policy	consults with the board when questions of interpretation arise on board policy	facilitates systematic board review and revision of policy-making process
C. provides the board with timely information	does not provide the board with timely information needed for effective board decision making	assures that the board receives necessary information in a timely way, including relevant laws, policies, and procedures from local, state, and federal mandate	assists board in understanding the multiple perspectives surrounding issues, as well as possible implications of decisions	collaborates with the board to review and improve the effectiveness of information and guidance provided to the board

D. treats all board members fairly, respectfully, and responsibly	favors certain board members or is unresponsive to board members' perspectives on educational issues	treats all board members fairly, respectfully, and responsibly	facilitates resolution of concerns or conflicts through board dialogue that creates greater mutual understanding	increases board capacity through trust, encouragement, and personal example
E. provides necessary support for effective board decision-making	does not establish and implement effective procedures for board meetings	assures that the board has the necessary materials, information, and logistical support to make effective decisions	works with the board to assure that meeting agendas are focused and consistent with board priorities	collaborates frequently with the board to evaluate and improve the effectiveness of board decision making
F. builds strong team relationships with the board	does not attempt to establish a working team relationship with board	collaborates with board to develop structures, procedures, and norms for working as a team	works with board to monitor team effectiveness and adjust procedures accordingly	facilitates development of a board-superintendent team characterized by candor, deep listening, a collaborative spirit, and openness to change

Few roles in our society compare with a superintendent. Often, superintendents are CEOs of the largest, most complex organization in a community. Even board members that come from a career in education may have little understanding of the pressure, complexity, and sophistication of the superintendent's job. Superintendent frameworks with standards for evaluation help to define the role.

School board members can also play an important role in selecting evaluation criteria. Recent research in Washington State provides insight into the factors and sources of information boards consider when they evaluate a superintendent.[2] The top three factors that board members considered were financial management, communication, and effective working relationship with others. Figure 8.2 illustrates their responses to fourteen factors.

Figure 8.2 Ranking of factors considered by school board members when evaluating a superintendent

Factor	Very important	Somewhat important	Not important
Financial management	98%	2%	0%
Communication	97%	3%	0%
Working relationships	96%	4%	0%
District safety	91%	9%	0%
Goal accomplishment	90%	9%	1%
Community engagement	89%	11%	0%
Achievement data	88%	12%	0%
Leadership	87%	12%	1%
Graduation rates	81%	17%	2%
Community satisfaction	81%	18%	1%
Parent satisfaction	79%	20%	1%
Bond or levy passage	73%	21%	6%
Condition of facilities	67%	32%	1%
Student satisfaction	67%	31%	2%

In Washington, where 25–35 percent of a district's budget comes from local taxes, board members place a high priority on financial stewardship. Washington board members also place an emphasis on communication and working relationships. Forty percent of Washington board members have children in their school district, and more than one-third have worked in education. All of this affects how boards view the superintendent's performance and what they consider during evaluation.

Board Members' Role

Elected board members bring a variety of strengths that can help support improved district performance.

- **Community expertise:** no one knows their communities better than they do.
- **Trusted officials:** district voters placed their confidence in them.
- **Citizen expertise:** engaged, registered voters, and contributors to society.
- **Knowledge:** knowing what it takes to improve student learning.

It is critical to a fair and useful superintendent evaluation that board members understand their individual role and that of the board as a whole. However, when new board members and superintendents assume positions in a district, they may not share an understanding of their roles. This can make it difficult to function as a unit and provide clear guidance for the superintendent.

Lack of a shared understanding of roles can create confusion for a school district. A misunderstanding of roles can incline board members toward either micromanagement or inadequate oversight. If board members think their role is to run operations of the school district, keep everyone happy, and personally ensure the safety and success of every child and staff member, they may have a hard time setting consistent direction. Effective board members understand their role as setting policy, providing oversight, and establishing long-term goals and vision for the district.

Board Members' Responsibility

Responsibility here does not refer to a list of duties—that is, to responsibilities in the plural. Responsibility is a moral virtue that explains to whom and for what a person feels a sense of obligation or duty. Board members are stewards of the public's two most precious resources—their children and their money. Board members see financial management as the number one factor in superintendent evaluation (see figure 8.2). At the same time, board members see students, parents, and voters as their top responsibility (see figure 8.3). Differing perspectives on board members' responsibility can contribute to challenging board-superintendent relationships. On the other hand, responsibility is a critical component for board members' leadership.

Board members demonstrate responsibility when they face choices, understand the consequences, and select options to produce good outcomes. In this accountability era, it is helpful to acknowledge that external accountability is what people talk about when they believe others are not behaving responsibly. While the overwhelming majority of school board members are responsibly fulfilling their duties, the variance of opinion as to whom, for what, and to what extent they are responsible can create challenges among the governance team.

How board members think about their responsibility influences how they evaluate a superintendent. If board members think of themselves as responsible for the physical well-being of students, they may have increased interest in evaluating

Figure 8.3 Objects of responsibility by school board members in Washington State

	Very important	Somewhat important	Not important
Students	96%	4%	0%
Parents	96%	4%	0%
Voters	93%	7%	0%
Superintendent	93%	7%	0%
Minority groups	92%	8%	0%
Fellow board members	88%	12%	0%
Business and employers	56%	42%	2%
State government	49%	45%	6%
Federal government	34%	55%	11%

the superintendent based on the safety and security of students. If they think of themselves as responsible for the working conditions of staff, they might be more interested in input from staff members than in the concerns of parents, students, or constituents. If board members consider themselves responsible for improving nutrition, and emphasize that in their election, they may be more interested in the school lunch program than in improvement to learning and teaching.

Board members feel responsible to a wide variety of stakeholders—from students and parents to state and federal governments. Many board members and superintendents cite their primary objective as educating children to their full potential.[3] Some may see themselves as accountable for student performance on tests intended to measure knowledge and application of mathematics and literary skills.[4] Alternatively, a community may hold board members accountable for educating children with the social and citizenship skills necessary for sustaining a democratic society. School boards constantly seek to balance the public good and the good of individual students. Moe[5] called this conflict "one of the ironies of democracy: the schools have difficulty contributing to the quality of democratic government precisely because they are democratically controlled."

Education in a Democracy

Superintendent evaluation occurs within an international, national, state, and local context. Many variables are outside the control of the district, yet they affect perceptions of performance. The media and advocacy groups can influence the disposition of board members. In addition, board members bring their own experiences and background to the evaluation. Superintendent evaluation in this tension of competing priorities can seem unfair, inconsistent, and unpredictable.

Our democratic way of life is in constant tension between control and resistance.[6] Scholars discuss three competing purposes for public education—democratic equality, social efficiency, and social mobility.[7] Superintendent evaluation is an integral part of the political dynamics. Researchers have noted that in spite of training for boards and superintendents, their relationship is often challenged by the political context and shifting of power that is inherent in education governance.[8] This tension in public school governance affects board-superintendent relationships and the superintendent evaluation. The political role of a superintendent in allocating scarce resources can set up the governance for team conflict.

Sources of Information

Whom are board members listening to and where do they get information about the superintendent's performance? One of the most frequent sources of information for board members is their superintendent. A majority of board members (56.1 percent) "almost always" turn to their superintendent to get the information they need when making decisions; including those who do so "often" as well, the number is 88.7 percent.[9] Since superintendents are this valued by board members for information, there could be tension, conflicts of interest, or lack of full disclosure regarding the information board members receive. Superintendents knowingly or unknowingly may present some information while withholding other information.

Washington State school board members cited the superintendent as a very important source they considered when evaluating the superintendent. They cite personal observation as the source of information they considered in their recent evaluation of the superintendent. Figure 8.4 displays the sources of information they considered when evaluating a superintendent.[10]

Figure 8.4 Sources board members consider when evaluating a superintendent

Source of information	Very important	Somewhat important	Not important
Personal observation	90%	8%	2%
Superintendent	85%	14%	1%
Fellow board members	80%	19%	1%
District administrators	79%	21%	0%
Parents and community	75%	24%	1%
District teachers	75%	24%	1%
State test scores	71%	28%	1%
Other district staff	64%	34%	2%
Students	52%	44%	4%

PRACTICAL STEPS TO IMPROVING
SUPERINTENDENT EVALUATION

Recognizing that it can be challenging for a board and superintendent to conduct a fair and helpful superintendent evaluation, there are practical steps every team can take. Figure 8.5 outlines some of these steps.

Number one, *have a plan*. Improving the quality and value of superintendent evaluation in your district will not happen by itself. Apply a framework (rubric) to gauge the superintendent's performance by a progression of criteria, as figure 8.1 illustrates. Many states, in a collaborative effort of school boards associations and superintendents associations, have developed instruments and procedures to assist with evaluation. These are widely available through your school boards association and online. Your plan should include using a modern, best-practice approach and instrument. Keep in mind that a quality evaluation has more to do with the conversation that takes place among the board and together with the superintendent than the instrument used. Meaningful evaluation is not about a point in time dictated by policy, law, or practice. It is an *ongoing conversation* about the performance of the superintendent and outcomes of the school district.

The practice of *no surprises* is critical for a useful evaluation. Fairness and trust begin with a shared understanding of what is expected. Clarifying expectations is the top priority of effective teamwork. A clear and honest conversation with

Figure 8.5   Promising practices for superintendent evaluation

1. Plan your work. Intentional practice regarding superintendent evaluation strengthens your relationship and improves the quality of the evaluation.
2. Apply a framework for evaluation with clear and progressive descriptions of performance.
3. Schedule a periodic, year-round discussion of expectations and progress focused on improvement.
4. Develop clear and shared expectations in advance about the criteria for evaluation.
5. Use multiple sources and multiple data points that are clear and specific to determine progress.
6. Encourage reflective self-evaluation by the superintendent.
7. Ensure the alignment the superintendent's job description, district goals, superintendent goals, other district employee evaluations, and the board's self-assessment.
8. Create a respectful, collegial, and consultative relationship between the board and superintendent.

written notes of the agreements at the start of the *evaluation cycle* builds trust and commitment among the team. This is not a one-time conversation. The conversation about performance is an ongoing item in the board's work with the superintendent. Many states allow for a private or closed session when it comes to discussing the superintendent's performance, but it is much better to happen in public than for it not to happen at all. Some boards are making this a monthly or quarterly agenda item at a regular board meeting. Others are building the discussion about performance into retreats, work sessions, and special meetings. Regardless of the time and place, get it on the calendar.

The criteria for performance evaluation needs to be crystal clear. If the team is going to use objective measures, everyone needs to know what those are and commit to applying the agreed sources of data and indicators to measure the progress. Fuzzy notions like "improve student learning," "make the teachers happy," or "improve the budget" are not only unclear but also likely to result in an ineffective evaluation and unproductive district outcomes. When the board and superintendent are clear about the outcomes and measures, the system has the opportunity to deliver improved results.

If the board and superintendent agree to improve student learning, then a clear and agreed measure of success might be to improve reading scores as measured by DIBELS by 1.5 percent in the fourth grade this year. While many factors may contribute to this accomplishment, the board is setting the expectation and measuring the performance of the superintendent by their ability to lead the system to make this gain. If the board wants to increase the district's reserves, the board might express the expectation to improve the ending fund balance this year by 0.5 percent. In doing so, the board and the superintendent need to understand together in advance the factors of that goal that are within the superintendent's control and factors such as weather or mechanical issues that are not.

INCREASING EVALUATION EFFECTIVENESS

We know more than ever before what makes for effective superintendents, school boards, and school districts. Board members, according to one recent survey, are highly committed to making a difference for students. One of the best ways to do that may be improving their evaluation of a superintendent. Improving superintendent evaluation can start with updating job descriptions, setting measurable goals, and adopting a research-based evaluation framework.

Updating the Job Description

The superintendent's role has changed dramatically. Superintendents used to be responsible for the "killer B's"—buildings, buses, budgets, and bonds. Today, they are responsible for student growth, teacher evaluation, student assessment, and increasing graduation rates. Updating the superintendent's job description is an easy place to start. A research-based superintendent framework with standards for evaluation provides a great foundation. A board and superintendent can meet in a work session to customize the job description, based on your district priorities. Then, align your evaluation system with the job description.

Setting Measureable Goals

The Lighthouse study[11] shows the importance of selecting two to three specific, long-term (three- to five-year) goals with a focus on student achievement. While board perspectives vary widely, boards might consider the following items:

- **Growth goals for the superintendent:** Ask the superintendent to complete a self-assessment based on a research-based framework. From that, the superintendent selects an area for professional skill development. One example might be to improve communications skills in support of a specific initiative. This growth goal can improve district leadership over time.
- **District goals:** Districts often have strategic plans, improvement plans, or specific goals. Examples include (a) improve the ending fund balance, (b) adopt a new math curriculum, or (c) implement a new teacher evaluation system. Often these goals can make the organization stronger but may not directly improve student learning.
- **Student achievement goals:** Federal rules require all districts to set Annual Measurable Objectives for student growth. The Annie E. Casey Foundation and others suggest that "leading indicators"—like proficiency in third-grade reading—are highly predictive of high school graduation. Reviewing student

achievement gaps is an excellent way to select a few measurable, high-impact student learning goals for the district.

Setting goals is an area where board members' understanding of roles and their responsibility may come into conflict. Some members may want a greater focus on *relationships*. These board members may prefer goals like improved communication or public involvement in a math adoption. Other boards may feel more responsible for *results*. These board members may prefer outcome measures like the ending fund balance and improved test scores. Acknowledging this tension can enable boards and superintendents to select an acceptable mix of goals that meet priorities for both relationship *and* results.

Boards navigating this balance should be aware that relationships and monitoring results are both critical to an effective board. It might surprise some board members that relationships among board members, with their community, and with their superintendent are more important than they realized. In fact, research indicates that board effectiveness in improving student achievement cannot be achieved by focusing exclusively on outcomes-based monitoring; relationship is critical.[12]

Adopting a Research-Based Evaluation Framework

New research-based frameworks for superintendent evaluation are based on national research and modeled after teacher evaluation frameworks now adopted in nearly every state. Often these frameworks have four to six research-based criteria with several indicators under each. The indicators have a four-part rubric that shows a progression from basic or non-satisfactory to proficient and distinguished.

DESCRIBING THE SUPERINTENDENT EVALUATION FRAMEWORK

Getting Started

Superintendent evaluations can make an important difference in student achievement. Starting any new process takes time and feels awkward in the beginning. That can cause resistance—from the board, the superintendent, or both. That said, there are ways to make implementing a new process less challenging.

Incremental Process.   A district can move into the evaluation process gradually. You might choose to update your job description and add a few indicators to your existing evaluation form in year one. The next year, you could add some student achievement goals to your existing evaluation. In the next few years, you might begin using one of the frameworks for evaluation, starting with the highest priority area for your district. A gradual approach gives the board and superintendent an opportunity to grow into evaluation standards and processes.

A New Culture.   This kind of superintendent evaluation is more than just a new tool. To be effective, the evaluation process can cultivate a new way of learning and doing. School boards that start by creating a comprehensive change all at once often find that overwhelming. This new approach can improve their entire way of working together and promote a more engaged and intentional governance process. District goals and student achievement begin to drive everything that the board does. Yes, it may take several work sessions to agree to goals and the evaluation framework. However, that process brings clarity to the work of the board and superintendent. The board may start asking for more updates on district goals—through work sessions, regular meetings, or written reports. The board will eventually want to change the budget process to align with the district goals. As staff and community notice the priorities and align their work, student achievement begins improving. This work takes time. It is not accomplished overnight.

Making It Work

Agree on Goals.   This can be the most difficult part of the process. Board members often feel strongly about their perspectives and priorities. Most boards need to hire someone to facilitate this process. A good facilitator can help ensure all points of view are heard and help the team reach agreement. It is OK to give yourselves some time. This is hard work. Jim Collins, in the bestseller *Good to Great*, says it takes an average of four years of refinement to align good goals, strategies, and measures. Again, take your time. It is worth the effort.

One strategy that school districts, as well as other organizations, are using is to develop *SMART goals*, as described below. SMART goals can be acted upon and easily understood. However, just as with other aspects of improvement, this is an iterative process—meaning, no one gets them perfect the first time. You want to refine them each year.

- **Specific:** Something like "increase third-grade proficiency in reading by 10%" is far better than the more generic "increase student achievement in math."
- **Measurable:** This is difficult. Areas such as test scores or budget balances are easier to measure. Others, such as community involvement, are more difficult to measure. Give yourself time to get it right.
- **Achievable:** Set some goals that can lead to "quick wins." This keeps momentum and commitment growing.
- **Resources:** Make sure that you have enough time and money to accomplish the needed strategies.
- **Time Bound:** Establish the time frame, e.g., "By October 30 we will . . ." or "By June 1 we will . . .".

Take time to develop SMART goals that are clear, concise, and well thought out. Avoid the temptation to lump several goals into one superordinate goal.

Strategies and Outcomes.   Human nature seems to favor either lots of activities *or* specific outcomes. Both are important, and they need to connect with each other. Saying we will increase test scores by 10 percent with no strategies in mind is a wish and a prayer, not a goal. Saying we will train all teachers in the new evaluation system without outlining what the teachers will be able to do is unlikely to produce results. A goal and strategy that are well connected is much better. *If we* provide professional development in specific ELL vocabulary strategies, *then* we will close the achievement gap for ELL students by 10 percent over the next year. Remember, hope is not a strategy.

Calendar the Work.   As indicated above, this is hard work and it takes time. Set aside one work-study a month to work on these evaluation and goal-setting ideas. Make an annual schedule that includes deadlines for goal setting, agreement on the evaluation process, midyear and end-of-year review. Put the dates on your board calendar. Hire a facilitator. Make and keep commitments.

Who Does What. This is new work, and it is normal to feel uncertain. Talk about who does what. Will the superintendent carry the responsibility for all this work? Will he or she work with the board chair or a committee of the board? Who will initiate the work? Some boards ask the superintendent to assemble the evidence (on the goals and rubric) and do an initial self-assessment. Others ask a committee of the board to meet with the superintendent and review evidence of success; some add ratings and others do not. Some boards ask each individual board member to review the data and compile individual ratings to be added together by the board chair. Our experience is that the process is most valuable when it is OK to engage in rich and deep conversations, and everyone understands that this is a work in progress. Get data to board members well in advance and ask them to study it in advance. If you ask board members to rank scores in advance, consider dropping the high score and low score to focus on the consensus of the board. Allow enough time for in-depth conversation among board members and the superintendent—the conversation is more valuable than the rating. Ask the board chair to summarize the consensus of the board in the final write-up of the evaluation.

CONCLUSION

While improving superintendent evaluation can be a challenging endeavor, we believe it is both needed and worth the effort. Your state school boards and superintendents associations have resources that can assist any district in improving this process. If not, they can point out where to find the resources you need. All of this is about improving outcomes for students. We trust that those engaged in the work of school governance are committed to improving everything you do, and we believe you and your students will benefit from improving superintendent evaluation in your district.

PART III

Putting It All Together

Balanced Governance in Action

9

The Panasonic Foundation Experience

Promising Practices and Lessons Learned
from Work with Urban School Boards

Andrew Gelber and Scott Thompson

The Panasonic Corporation of North America established the Panasonic Foundation in 1984 to give something back to the United States by helping to improve public education. The Foundation's mission is "to partner with public school districts and their communities to break the links between race, poverty, and educational outcomes by improving the academic and social success of ALL students: ALL MEANS ALL." The Foundation's distinctive approach includes engagement with school boards, superintendents, and professional unions/associations in each district with which we partner. In these partnerships, the Foundation provides direct assistance through the work of experienced education consultants rather than making grants as so many philanthropic foundations do. Over the years, the Foundation has partnered with more than thirty-five school districts, in most parts of the United States.[1]

Over the past twenty-eight years working with urban school boards, it has become clear to us that these boards need to know and be able to do certain things to be highly effective drivers, stewards, and champions of a system that improves achievement for all students. In this chapter, we share key lessons learned and promising practices observed in this work.

The Panasonic Foundation has learned that working to improve a board's ability to carry out its roles effectively represents a high-leverage strategy for advancing the Foundation's equity mission. Helping school boards and superintendents to clarify and calibrate their respective roles and responsibilities makes a significant contribution to the district's capacity to achieve better student outcomes. We have learned that a superintendent cannot successfully pursue an equity-focused agenda in the absence of robust support from the school board. Also, the roles of stewardship (of values and resources) and advocacy (on behalf of students' needs) are unique to the school board. Finally, we have come to understand that as the school board sits at the intersection of the *inside* of the school system (its instructional core of teaching and learning) and the *outside* of the system (its wider community context), it is uniquely placed to moderate or filter the impact of the latter on the former.

While it is clear that highly effective school boards can make a critical contribution toward improving student achievement in their districts, it has been our observation that good boardsmanship remains an uncommon phenomenon. Reasons for this probably include that, as elected or politically appointed officials, school board members often operate with a mental model based on political/legislative bodies and seldom understand the inappropriateness of that model for school system governance. Secondly, the difference between the school board's governance/policy role and the superintendent's administration/management role is often poorly understood. Finally, effective professional development for school boards is rare. These elements are all important in supporting a Balanced Governance approach to board operations.

If school boards are going to be highly effective, making a critical contribution to educational excellence and equity, they need to be able to specify the school system's expected results for student achievement (asking themselves, for example, what would characterize a well-prepared high school graduate in their system), and they need to monitor the system's progress toward achieving those expected results. School boards need to direct the system's resources toward the accomplishment of the expected results. They need to ask thoughtful questions about how (and how well) the system's strategies, programs, and practices are contributing toward the accomplishment of the expected results. It is the responsibility of the school board to articulate the core values and vision that drive the system as well as to cross-reference those core values and vision as they go about making policy decisions. It is important that school boards understand the difference between their role (policy/governance) and the superintendent's role (administration/management), and they need to respect the importance of not going *below the line* that separates those roles and domains. Finally, school board members must understand how to function as a whole board, recognizing the need for compromise and doing what is in the best interest of the entire district rather than representing specific constituencies and personal agendas.

A board that understands and stays true to its governance role still may not be able to create a high performing school system with a strong focus on student achievement. There are additional indispensable success factors. However, high-quality school governance is essential. When school boards behave badly—when they do not carry out their governance role—not only do they complicate and confuse the work of district and school leaders, but their actions often cascade down the system and show up in classrooms, adversely affecting student outcomes.

School boards need to think both about *what* they need to do and *how* they need to do it, since both dimensions of their work have a profound effect on everything and everyone else in the system. Put another way, school boards need to concern themselves both with *doing things right* and with *doing the right things*. If they do not do things right, their work will be ineffective and inefficient. If they do not do the right things, the specific contributions that only the board can make toward the improvement of student achievement will not occur, and the district's efforts on behalf of its students will be compromised.

DOING THE RIGHT THINGS

School systems exist to educate all students to high levels. The essential mission of a school board is to govern the school system on behalf of its community as a whole. As the guardian of its community's schools, the board serves as a trustee acting on behalf of current citizens *and* future citizens. Christa McAuliffe, the Teacher-in-Space who died in the Challenger Space Shuttle explosion, once said, "I touch the future, I teach." School boards shape the future. Their actions affect the quality of education for all of their community's children, and hence those children's capacities for productive citizenship in the decades to come. It is critical for boards to "do the right things" because, if the board does not perform the duties that constitute its role in the school system, there is no one else who can perform them. There are critical roles and responsibilities on behalf of improving student achievement that only the board can accomplish. These roles and responsibilities lie at the heart of doing the right things. School boards need to own, steward, and champion the district's vision and values for student achievement.

Board-Superintendent Partnership

Many school boards believe that their number one responsibility is to hire a good superintendent and let him or her do whatever needs to be done. They think that the superintendent should set the vision and the board should adopt it. Morally, however, the board must actively participate in determining the vision and values of the district because they are ultimately responsible to the community.

The Panasonic Foundation has found that the best context for improving student achievement occurs when the school board and superintendent are both unwavering in their vision of a better district and conscious that they are mutually dependent for making that vision a reality. The board must develop a clear, compelling, and energizing vision, not hollow platitudes that are passed off as vision statements. If the vision is mundane or muddled, then all of the aligning and guiding that follow are tied to a flawed point of reference.

Setting Board Values

A board must articulate what it believes in and stands for—its fundamental values. The board cannot be silent or neutral in this area. Values exist, whether articulated or not, and will drive board actions. Board members represent their community, which is likely to have competing, even conflicting values. In the boardroom, the community's different perspectives and values should be discussed and consensus reached on what *this* board believes in and stands for. Then, the board must make explicit pronouncements on what it values—what it sees as acceptable and unacceptable. These values will form the framework for actions by the board and staff. Articulating the board's values makes it possible for everyone in the district to use the same compass for the countless daily decisions that push (or pull) a district toward its vision. It is not sufficient, though, for a school board simply to develop a clear vision and a set of values. School boards need to use their adopted vision and values actively and consistently as a guide for all policy development, decision making, and budgeting.

School boards have many policies handed to them by federal or state authorities. However, the board often has authority to adapt federal or state policies to meet local needs, and often is in a position to promulgate local policies based on its own vision, values, and objectives. In areas that the school board has authority regarding policies, it should ask itself the following questions about those policies:

- How well do the policies align with and communicate its vision, values, and objectives?
- Are all policies written, codified, and easily accessible to board and staff?
- How clearly do the policies provide guidance to the superintendent and staff about what they can and cannot do in achieving the board's vision, values, and objectives?
- How well do the policies provide guidance to the board itself?
- Are all policies sufficiently clear such that the superintendent can operate within those policies and have, in effect, "prior board approval?"
- Can any unclear policies be clarified to guide action without additional board approval?
- Do any policies impede staff in taking actions that are consistent with the board's vision, values, and objectives? If so, what policy changes must be made to remove those impediments?
- Does the board have an effective process for regularly reviewing and revising policies to achieve the desired results?

Avoiding Micromanagement

Boards sometimes feel that they have to cover every contingency and make explicit in advance what staff should do. Their policies read like procedure manuals and become even more prescriptive every time there is an incident in which staff action is unacceptable to the board. Instead of micromanaging staff actions, boards should make it clear, through policies, what staff may *not do*—what is unethical or simply unacceptable to the board given its beliefs and values. Be as specific as necessary for the board to feel comfortable that staff actions, within those limits, are already approved.

Articulating limits through policies requires more up-front board work but saves board time later by not requiring review of an unending list of proposed staff actions. By using a limits approach to policy, the board is in effect telling staff, "Do whatever you think will work best, within the boundaries we have set." Staff members are more accountable under this approach because there is no impediment to their being proactive in finding the best way to achieve the expected results. The worst situation is for a school board to have unclear or inconsistent policies and to constantly review staff actions. Some boards act as if they prefer this. They avoid the tough, board-level work of creating clear, consistent board policies and instead focus on individual staff actions.

Commitment to Equity

While different boards will necessarily promote different values, we believe that certain values are nonnegotiable and ought to be promoted by all school boards. We believe that all boards should commit to the mission of breaking links between race, poverty, and educational outcomes. This represents a systemwide commitment to equity and excellence. While different districts may present different equity challenges, and different boards may develop customized, district-specific definitions of equity, we believe that a clear commitment to make good on the promise of "all means all" is an absolute necessity. In addition, having adopted a values-driven commitment to equity, the board must find ways to use actions, as well as words, to realize that commitment.

The Panasonic Foundation project described in this chapter recognizes that an equity-focused mission can create controversies for both boards and superintendents. Therefore, we did everything possible to help boards and superintendents in our partner districts deal effectively with controversies and challenges when they arose. As a way of expressing the dedication and energy this vision requires, we call upon school boards and superintendents to be *equity warriors* on behalf of all students. Thus, as an essential component of doing the right things, school boards need to muster the political will to function as equity warriors on behalf of currently underachieving students. School boards can demonstrate commitment to "all means all" by championing educational excellence for all students and vigilantly attending to educational experiences and success of students who are underachieving historically or currently.

A school board focused on equity and excellence demonstrates its commitment to all students learning to high levels, not only through its vision, values, and expected results, but also in how it performs its duties. When monitoring results, an effective board seeks a range of evidence on how well each group of students is succeeding, at each phase of education in the district. It not only examines disaggregated test scores, but also looks at data on dropouts, attendance, disciplinary actions, enrollment in advanced as well as remedial classes, rates of failure in grades or subjects, and rates of continuous academic progress for students as they move through the system. The board also demonstrates its commitment by persistently pushing for better results among students who are falling behind.

In some districts, it requires a great deal of courage for the board to publicly discuss low-achievement results and insist on taking actions that address underlying problems and inequities. There can be a long history of inaction and considerable forces maintaining that inertia. The pervasive belief that "certain kids" cannot succeed in school may have long gone unchallenged. The community may have been accustomed to tolerating significant differences in quality between/among district schools, with some have-not schools serving most of the district's low-achieving students. There can be intense political pressures to place a Band-Aid over trouble spots. However, we have seen school boards take on these challenges, rise to the occasion, and refuse to accept excuses or permit exceptions to their expectation that *all* children will learn to high levels.

Importance of a Strategic Plan

Using the board's vision and values as the starting point, the superintendent and staff are charged with the development of a district strategic plan and accompanying work plans or action plans to support the implementation of specific strategies. The board's vision and values create vertical and horizontal parameters for the strategic plan and accompanying action plans. The vision focuses the district on what it should see as it looks up. The values tell the staff about the *outer walls*, and what must be within them—the acceptable and necessary things to do—and what must be outside of them because such actions would be unacceptable and/or unnecessary.

With these parameters in place, the board and superintendent can decide what the most important objectives to reach over the next few years are, and how they will determine success in meeting these objectives. It is incumbent upon the school board to articulate the results it expects to see (in student achievement particularly and in other areas of district progress more generally) and to establish, in collaboration with the superintendent, effective processes for monitoring progress toward those results.

Many boards set objectives; few boards are clear about what will constitute satisfaction of their objectives. Boards need to decide how they will assess progress and what criteria will determine the extent to which objectives are met. These objectives and criteria become the *expected district results*, for which the superintendent will be evaluated and held accountable.

Monitoring Progress

All boards know that it is their responsibility to watch what is happening in their districts and to be able to answer the question, "How are we doing?" Student test scores, particularly gains in achievement, are obviously a much-valued source of data about how a district is doing. However, effective boards know that more information is needed to assess the success of a district than viewing the end-of-the-year scoreboard of standardized test results.

In a typical district, staff members satisfy the board's duty to monitor progress by supplying a constant stream of data on what the district is doing—everything from kindergarten skills assessments to school bus maintenance schedules. In a typical district, boards dutifully speed-read mounds of staff reports and find information that enables each member to answer the question, "How are we doing?" The board in a typical district can in some sense be said to be fulfilling its duty to articulate expected results and monitor progress. But, this typical board has not made it clear *what* it will watch and *how good* the results must be if they are to be judged satisfactory.

Being up-front with expected results and criteria for evaluation is hard work and time-consuming. Nevertheless, this up-front investment pays off over the long run, including these benefits:

- Increasing the board's ability to control its agenda. Every meeting agenda doesn't have to start "from scratch" with the chairperson and superintendent trying to figure out what the board needs to hear about this time.
- Focusing the information that comes to the board on board-level interests, not staff-level interests. Improving board judgment by providing more concise and focused reports telling the board about what it cares most in a way that facilitates informed decisions around the results.
- Saving board time for areas needing special attention.
- Saving staff and board members time spent preparing for meetings.
- Eliminating window-dressing staff reports that focus only on what is going well while glossing over poor results.

Sustainability

School boards need to take responsibility and ownership for the sustainability of the district's strategic direction, so that it is carried forward when the superintendency changes. Focus on sustainability is a critical board responsibility for at least two reasons. In the first instance, focus derives from the board's leadership role for developing, articulating, owning, and promoting the district's vision, values, and expected results. While these can occasionally be revisited and revised, they should not be "flavor-of-the-month" priorities but rather long-standing, defining aspects of the district's aims and aspirations. As such, they should not be up for grabs as part of the process of seeking and hiring a new superintendent but should rather function as givens to which a prospective superintendent is or is not attracted. It is important for a board to seek and nurture compatibility with a newly hired superintendent, but that compatibility should derive from the superintendent endorsing and sharing the vision and values sustained and expressed by the board, not from the board relinquishing its vision-setting role.

The second reason for the critical importance of the board's focus on sustainability is the short tenure of many superintendents, especially in urban districts. In order to avoid the harmful phenomenon of forcing the system to change vision and direction with every change in executive leadership, the board needs to protect and shepherd the defining components of the district's vision, values, and expected results through these predictable changes in the superintendency.

Fiscal Responsibilities

Policies and allocation of fiscal resources are powerful tools the board uses to achieve the district's vision, values, and desired results. In the absence of a vision- and values-driven guiding framework, political pressures of the here and now often drive decisions about policies, and about budgets and fiscal allocations, and not what best serves the long-term objectives for student achievement. A board driven by its vision of all children succeeding in all schools adopts a budget that allocates resources based on schools' and students' needs, not artificial formulas or customary allocations. The board must not be afraid to provide significantly greater resources to low-performing schools, especially when constituents of those schools are not politically powerful members of the community.

A board's fiscal responsibilities do not end once a budget is approved. It must have policies and processes to monitor and maintain financial management that achieves the board's vision for academic improvement. The board should be able to tell the public regularly and effectively that its money is being well spent in the schools. Finally, a responsible board is able to build public support for revenue increases when such funding is essential to having schools in which all students learn.

An important component of the board's budget/fiscal responsibilities is its leadership in negotiating and approving union contracts. What gets decided at contract time can greatly help or hinder a district's capacity to achieve its objectives. Boards can lose sight of the fact that a contract is another way of setting policy, and that contractual obligations can preempt or conflict with other policies. Boards must foreground their vision, values, and objectives as they make compromises needed for an approvable contract.

Finally, the school board needs to take a leadership role in building and maintaining community-wide commitment, respect, and trust regarding the overall educational enterprise of the school district. The school board has a great influence on its district's culture and climate. The actions it takes—or fails to take—can make or break an effective organizational culture. The climate of commitment, trust, and respect that it nourishes—or diminishes—lays the groundwork for the success or failure of its vision and goals for student success.

DOING THINGS RIGHT

Doing things right is the procedural side of the equation stated earlier in this chapter, and success in this endeavor makes it more likely that the board will ultimately succeed in doing the right things. So, what are some of the things that the board needs to do right?

Disciplined Processes

School boards need to develop, and consistently apply, a coherent set of disciplined processes for doing their work. These include basic items, such as the procedures and timetables for agenda setting and the rules of order governing board meetings. Some boards define more complex processes, such as consistent talking points for members to use with constituents and defining roles and expectations for board and administrator interactions. Some boards develop processes to help members identify key questions related to upcoming administration presentations, so responses to questions are built into the presentation.

Among any board's disciplined processes should be the development of a *work plan*. The district's overall strategic plan is an essential element for progress toward student achievement, but it is not intended to guide the board work. This board work plan focuses on how the board uses its areas of authority (policy, budget, etc.) to contribute to accomplishing the district's vision.

School boards have a responsibility to engage the community in the success of the district. Boards have a responsibility to understand the beliefs and values of their communities, and they have an obligation to help shape those values and beliefs, as needed, to ensure educational equity and excellence.

Board-Superintendent Roles

As an essential component of doing things right, school boards need to develop and implement effective tools for evaluating their work as a board and evaluating the performance of the superintendent. As part of developing its work plan, the school board should establish criteria for assessing its progress and effectiveness and assessing the extent to which its objectives have been met. The school board holds itself accountable for completing its work and accomplishing what only it can do to achieve overall district objectives.

School boards are typically conscious of their supervisory role over their chief executive—the superintendent. Most school boards strongly value a good relationship with the superintendent. Difficulties can arise, however, when school boards (a) do not clearly define what they will hold the superintendent accountable for, (b) are ineffective in monitoring superintendent performance, or (c) intrude in ways that make it difficult to hold the superintendent accountable.

In order to overcome these difficulties, the board needs to define, and distinguish between, the superintendent's and the school board's roles and areas of responsibility. In a majority of districts, the chief executive goes by the title superintendent. It is helpful to consider the implications of the term "chief executive," however, because it helps to differentiate roles and responsibilities. The chief executive is the one who holds staff accountable—who is the boss of all staff. The chief executive *executes*, doing whatever it takes (within the limits of board policy) to ensure that desired results are achieved.

The separation between board and staff functions is unfortunately fuzzy in many districts. However, that line becomes distinct when the board focuses on fulfilling its responsibilities and has clear and explicit performance expectations and standards for itself and its chief executive. Board-staff separation becomes a problem when the board shirks its duties and tries to run the district. An effective board focuses on being the supervisor of one person and holding this person accountable. Further, an effective board operates as a unit, and the chief executive is clearly accountable to the whole board, not individual members.

School board intrusion into staff-level concerns is bad practice, because it muddies accountability. How can the superintendent be accountable for actions of staff members who acted under board direction? If those staff actions prove ineffective, will the superintendent be able to hold the board accountable? How would that work?

School boards need to monitor the chief executive's performance based on pre-established criteria. An effective board articulates clear expectations and performance standards for itself, for its chief executive, and for the board's work with this individual. The board establishes performance expectations for the superintendent using a clear set of criteria for evaluating performance. In addition, the board regularly reviews performance and determines if the superintendent is meeting performance targets.

The board should expect the superintendent to establish performance expectations for all other staff and have processes for determining how well staff members meet expectations. An effective board never tries to determine if other staff, below the level of the chief executive, are or are not meeting their performance expectations. This is the chief executive's responsibility.

Setting District Climate

The school board needs to take a leadership role in establishing a districtwide climate of trust and respect. Showing commitment to student success must be coupled with building a climate of trust and respect. Why? Because real, sustainable improvement in student learning only comes when there is a climate of trust and respect among the school board, superintendent, and staff.

Even with boards with good intentions, we have seen board actions that significantly damage trust and respect. Most notably, some boards allow individual members to publicly criticize staff. Effective school boards are respectful in interactions with staff. They demonstrate this in how they listen to and ask questions of staff. Because an effective board needs to be able to trust the information used to make decisions, they encourage staff to be open and honest in their reports and in board-staff discussions. Such boards eliminate actions that make staff regret having been open and honest with the board.

Effective boards insist on a proper use of authority and behavior befitting their position as the community's trustees for children and their education. They establish a code of conduct for the board and its members and have clearly understood processes and consequences that hold the board and its members accountable. One of the key principles in this code is a clear distinction between the board as a whole and individual members. Only the board, acting as a body, has authority. Thus, individual members may not attempt to exercise authority over the superintendent or staff, and may not speak for the board, unless specifically granted this power by the board as a whole.

Conflict happens; it is unavoidable. The problem for boards isn't having conflict among members' views and opinions, it is how to manage the conflict so that the exchange of ideas is productive and leads to good board policies and actions. A code of conduct establishes rules for dialogue, debate, and making decisions. When the board makes a decision, even when it is divided in the decision, the board has acted. In all subsequent interactions with the public, staff, and media, individual members must understand they have no authority to speak against what the board as a whole decided.

10

Learning the Work by Doing the Work

The Massachusetts District Governance Support Project

Dorothy Presser and Nancy Walser

In 2011, the state of Massachusetts applied for and received Race to the Top (RTTT) grant funding. In a unique move among grant recipients, the Massachusetts Department of Elementary and Secondary Education (DESE) allocated some of the grant funds for a project to build the governing capacity of school committees[1] to carry out their roles of positively impacting student achievement—the District Governance Support Project (DGSP).

The DGSP was created to complement another new program begun with RTTT funds, the New Superintendent Induction Program (NSIP)—a three-year program for first-time superintendents or superintendents new to Massachusetts. The purpose of NSIP is to help new superintendents develop the strategies and practices that will help them focus on and effectively address the issues that most affect teaching and learning in their district. By introducing the District Governance Support Project in conjunction with NSIP, state education officials hoped to amplify the impact that each program would have for a district.

A further impetus for the DGSP stemmed from the strong belief in Massachusetts in the essential role of local governance to represent the vision and values of local communities. School boards comprised of community members originated in the Commonwealth of Massachusetts and are viewed by many as an integral part of our American institution of representative governance. They epitomize democratic principles by giving parents and communities a voice in critical policy issues that affect their schools.

Another inspiration for the project was the growing body of research which indicates that high functioning school committees can positively influence student achievement. Conversely, a committee that does not understand its role in furthering student achievement and district goals could operate in ways that impede district progress and student outcomes. The theory of action for the DGSP is that if superintendents and school committees can build relationships, understand respective roles and responsibilities, and support each other's work, they will then be more successful at raising student achievement. In addition, the research has identified practices common to high functioning committees. The project sought to introduce these practices to participating committees with the belief that adopting the practices would have a positive impact.

The curriculum content in DGSP was informed by several of these research projects, some of which are covered in other chapters of this book, including the Lighthouse study, common practices of high functioning schools boards identified in Walser's *Essential School Board Book*, and the experience of the Panasonic Foundation in its work with urban districts over twenty-five years.

DGSP, therefore, is designed to give school committees the tools and practices they need to focus on student achievement and continuous improvement. The foundational beliefs of the program are as follows:

- The overarching mission of any school committee (board) is continuous improvement in student achievement.
- School committee practices are related to student achievement.
- The school committee and superintendent are a *governance team* in this mission.
- Effective leadership to support student achievement requires a good working relationship—a model for all others in the schools.
- A team learns to work together by doing the work after establishing norms or protocols.

DESIGNING THE PROGRAM

In 2011, a design team was formed to develop a curriculum for the District Governance Support Project. The team included two retired superintendents who were coaches in the NSIP, staff from the Massachusetts Association of School Committees (MASC), a project director, a DESE representative, and the two authors of this chapter.

The training envisioned by the design team was unique compared to most board training programs that were in place. The entire governance team—committee members and the superintendent—would participate in the training together. This would best enable the individual members to come together as a team, develop a common vision for the school district, and create common understandings of how they would work together. The training was designed as a series of workshops, not just a one-stop session, and the workshops built upon each other. The team would begin by discussing and agreeing *how* they would work together and practice these agreements as they explored and agreed upon *what* work needed to be accomplished for students in the district.

Anticipated Challenges

The design team knew that the time committees had to devote to the training would be a potentially limiting factor. There were two challenges: one was getting committees to commit the time necessary for the training, and the other was finding times that the entire group could come together to participate in the workshops. The coaches delivering the curriculum would have to accommodate the time that various committees had available. Every workshop was planned to be about two hours in length and take place about once a month. However, from the outset, program designers knew that coaches would have to offer different options, such as meeting more often for shorter periods of time before or after regular meetings, combining workshops into longer Saturday sessions, or spacing workshops at intervals around other committee obligations.

Perhaps the most important challenge was ensuring that the governance practices introduced in the program were sustainable over time and over changes in the governance team. While superintendents participating in NSIP could bring their learning to other districts if they moved on, the training of school committee members could be lost as those members who participated in the project stepped off the board. The curriculum needed to emphasize that the practices and procedures learned by committees could and should be revisited and continued in the future.

Yet an additional challenge was that no two committees are alike. They have different strengths, challenges, and philosophies—not to mention different numbers of members. Some may have already adopted some of the practices and work products the curriculum covered. Some were ready to hear what the curriculum had to offer and take off at a run. Others needed more support to understand the value and necessity of the work. The coaches who conducted the training had to be able to tailor the curriculum to the needs of a particular district and be able to adjust to the dynamics of different groups successfully.

As with any training, the right trainer contributes to the success of the venture. For the DGSP, the coaches who conduct the training are all former school committee members. The coaches have experience dealing with the very issues they talk to school committees about. They have experience dealing with constituent issues and crafting budgets in difficult fiscal environments. They have negotiated collective bargaining agreements and hired superintendents. They have had to develop relationships with colleagues and superintendents as well as an understanding of the dynamics of working on a local governing board. In other words, they brought not only experience, but also a level of credibility to the training. The primary goal of the DGSP was to help any committee adopt effective practices, no matter the starting point. It was important, therefore, that committees did not feel that this was remedial training. Coaching by someone who could be viewed as a colleague contributed to this effort.

The design team had no shortage of ideas about what information to include in the curriculum. In part because of the issues listed above, the curriculum was kept flexible, with lots of examples and ideas for coaches to choose from. In laying out the seven workshops/modules of the original pilot program, the design team used a consultant with a background in adult learning to lay out an agenda for each workshop that varied and would keep participants engaged. Materials in each module included PowerPoints to guide the discussion, case studies, in some cases video clips of school committee meetings to demonstrate a point or generate discussion, small group exercises, and examples of materials from other school committees. To address the need for flexibility of working with different committees, coaches were able to select from the available materials to plan their workshops.

IMPLEMENTATION

The Department of Elementary and Secondary Education selected the first cohort of committees to participate in the DGSP. They were districts that had new superintendents participating in NSIP and that faced significant student achievement challenges. Despite the fact that most of the districts were receiving specific interventions required by DESE, they were not required to participate in the DGSP—this truly was an invitation, which most districts chose to accept.

Once the coaches began working in districts, it became apparent that the design team was right on the money in some of the anticipated challenges. It was quickly apparent that tailoring the curriculum to a committee was important. Coaches needed to gain an understanding of the issues in a district, the protocols and dynamics that existed on the governance team, and what level of planning and goal development was already in place to engage a committee successfully. Without this understanding, planning a productive workshop would have been a difficult, if not impossible, exercise. This initial understanding was often gained by meeting with the committee chair and superintendent prior to the first workshop. In addition, coaches researched the district by looking at its Web site and the profile information on the district available on the state's Department of Elementary and Secondary Education Web site.

Time was indeed a precious commodity. In many instances, it was difficult to find a time when all members of a governance team could meet for a workshop. This meant that, often, not all team members were present at a workshop, so a voice was lost in the process. In addition, it was frequently difficult to schedule the workshops. The time between workshops varied greatly depending on the other commitments of the committees such as budget meetings and events that pulled on members' time. However, even though it took longer than anticipated, the vast majority of committees that began the program did see it through to the end.

Committees also had different ideas about what a good start time for the program would be. Some wanted to start after elections so that they knew the participating team would be in place for a while. Some committees were ready to dive right in when asked, others preferred to wait until after budgets had been settled or until after the end of the school year. In many respects, flexibility truly was an important attribute of the project's coaches.

As coaches began working with different committees, the library of curriculum materials grew. Coaches developed or sought out materials to present at various workshops that would be pertinent to a particular team. As committees developed work products, such as operating protocols or norms, coaches shared these with each other. Sifting through the material and deciding what to present became a time-consuming task for coaches. In addition, the curriculum presented to different districts became less consistent.

MAKING ADJUSTMENTS

As the third year of the program approached, it became apparent that the curriculum resulting from the work of the design team covered so much ground and provided so much choice of material that the coaches were spending hours just picking through the material to prepare for workshops. Coaches were struggling with the competing desires of tailoring the curriculum to local needs and having an easier-to-implement program that they could be confident would be helpful for their committees.

Based on work done with the Leominster School Committee, Nancy began posting the PowerPoints she had created on a wiki. Other coaches contributed material as well, and the authors were subsequently deputized by the project manager to streamline the curriculum into units that could be delivered in fifty hours, including five two-hour workshops, one-on-one coaching time with the board chair, and workshop prep and follow-up after each workshop with the chair, superintendent, and NSIP coach.

Before selecting what to include in the streamlined curriculum, the authors met with Jim Marini and Chris McGrath of the NSIP program to help identify which parts of the curriculum were considered critical to helping superintendents and school board members work more collaboratively. Like the original design team, Chris and Jim were in complete agreement that establishing operating protocols was foundational to getting boards and superintendents to work as leadership teams—a concept embedded in the Balanced Governance model. As our small group ruminated on the word *foundation*, we also realized that the word held other possibilities. School boards are very familiar with the details of building and renovating school facilities: advocating for necessary funding, watching various stages of construction, and attending groundbreakings and ribbon-cuttings. What if we built our program around this familiar metaphor? As corny as it might sound, likening our core curriculum to the building of a *governance schoolhouse* would make it more user-friendly and hopefully more memorable.

After much discussion, Chris and Jim helped us clarify the four remaining critical activities for boards and superintendents around which the workshops were built: setting goals (the frame), monitoring progress (the systems), planning effective meetings (the walls), and sustaining the work (the roof). These five activities, from foundation to roof, are described below under Building the Governance Schoolhouse.

Work Products

Early feedback from the pilot districts also spurred us to add another element that would become a cornerstone of the training. While board members certainly appreciated the content of the early workshops, the value of the time spent in informal discussion with each other came as a true revelation to some. A few members even questioned whether the workshops were legal because they were not in the format of a regular business meeting, even though they were duly called and posted for the public as stipulated under the state's open meeting law. There seemed to be something wrong about simply having a meeting to talk about how to work together. "We have never talked to each other outside a meeting," said one participating school committee member.

We discovered that by working together to craft documents like operating protocols, board members got to know each other better and working together became easier. To Nancy, this brought to mind a phrase that one of her graduate professors often used in reference to his observation that educators in training "learn the work by doing the work." School boards, too, it seemed, learned the work by doing the work.

Thus, sparked the idea of making sure that every workshop included the creation of a *work product*—something begun by the group during the workshop, refined by ad hoc or subcommittee during the intervening weeks, to be (ideally) finalized by the group at the beginning of the next workshop. By putting the focus on *the process*, the training would empower school committees to draw on their own resources (including the superintendent) to determine the district's direction, thus building capacity at the district level. In addition, by providing a structure that was iterative and could be revisited each year (the five elements of the governance school house), the hope was that the training might help institutionalize a new way of governing in each district.

BUILDING THE GOVERNANCE SCHOOLHOUSE

So how did the DGSP workshops finally come together and what do they contain? The curriculum itself consists of a set of PowerPoints with embedded activities, prompts for discussion, and in many cases, exemplars or examples of work products completed by other school boards. These we quickly realized had more relevance if they were created by school committees in Massachusetts, rather than coming from national examples. Fortunately, by the end of the pilot program, we had assembled at least two to three examples of each of the five products. With input from MASC staff, and coaches Jim and Chris, the PowerPoints and a corresponding coaches' workbook became the curriculum.

To help us and our boards determine whether the workshops made any difference in changing beliefs and practices, we also created a rubric. Similar to many rubrics used in education, this served a dual purpose of illustrating a continuum while also serving as a tool for self-evaluation (see figure 10.1).

Workshop 1: The Foundation

To lay the foundation, the first workshop is devoted to reviewing the research linking school board practices; an overview of the different, yet complementary roles of the superintendent and the board (as well as those of the board as a whole and individual board members); and the critical role of communication. We found a video of a squabbling board posted on YouTube and then posed these questions in a PowerPoint:

- If someone new to town (like a parent of a kindergartner) turned on cable TV and saw one of your meetings, how would you hope that they could describe it?
- What are the obstacles to achieving this vision?
- What agreements about ways of working would help?

This segues into the main activities of the workshop: taking an initial assessment of the committee using the governance rubric, reviewing examples of operating protocols, and beginning the discussion of crafting a set of their own protocols. This was the work product for Workshop 1. Before the meeting ends, coaches get a specific commitment from the committee about how the draft protocols will be refined prior to Workshop 2. The following question is also posed to set the stage for producing the next product: "What are your top two concerns about students in the district?" Members (and the superintendent) are asked to write each concern on a yellow "sticky note" and give them to the coach.

Workshop 2: The Frame

In creating Workshop 2, we had to cope with a development we had not anticipated at the beginning of the design process. In the intervening months, a new mandate took effect in the state that requires school committees to evaluate the superintendent every year based on a specific yearly cycle that begins with the superintendent presenting the committee with a self-evaluation and a set of recommended SMART goals for the district upon which they will be evaluated.[2]

The new system had its pluses and minuses. On one hand, it promised to eliminate the somewhat sloppy, subjective, last-minute evaluations superintendents sometimes had to endure from unorganized committees. However, the new system was overly complex (instructions on the state Web site total more than forty pages alone and feature a model evaluation rubric with a total of sixty-three standards, indicators, and elements), and there was widespread confusion on how this new system would fit together (if at all) with previous mandates for district and school improvement plans.

Figure 10.1 Governance rubric for continuous improvement

	1	2	3	4
Goals	The district has no overarching or annual goals for improving student outcomes.	The school committee has adopted overarching goals and the SUP and SC have agreed on annual goals for the district but they are not discussed that often. The goals may not have been voted on by the full board.	The SC and SUP have adopted overarching goals, have agreed on annual goals, and they are posted on the Web site. Once a year they are used by the SC to evaluate the SUP.	The SC has adopted overarching goals, the SUP and SC have agreed on annual goals, and the SUP has used these in creating an improvement strategy for the district. The goals are a frequent topic of discussion in the school community, and at SC meetings, where they often drive budget decisions and other policies.
Operating protocols	Individual members and the SUP communicate separately based on personal relationships and prior traditions. Some members may feel left out, or speak negatively in public about each member's and the board's decisions.	Because of some tension on the board, the superintendent and some members of the SC have talked about making some rules for working together, but they may not be written down and have not come to a vote.	The SUP and the SC Chair have developed some guidelines for how the SC and SUP will work and communicate with each other and with the public. Not all members follow them, however, and this sometimes causes problems.	The SC and the SUP have agreed to written operating protocols for the board and they are followed most of the time. Periodically, the SC and SUP come together to talk about how they are working and to make adjustments. Problems are addressed in private conversations or in informal (public) workshops or retreats. The level of trust between members and the superintendent is high.
Meetings	Meetings are not well planned, are long and sometimes contentious. Very little time is spent talking about student achievement. Members feel free to bring up new proposals at meetings, surprising other members and the SUP. Some members dominate and meetings often get "stuck" due to personal agendas.	In general, the SUP and SC Chair set the agenda and surprises are kept to a minimum. However, when there is a major improvement initiative, meetings can be long and contentious. Engaging the community in the decision, while desired, is not typical. SC members are not always prepared to contribute with thoughtful questions.	The SUP and SC have an agreement on how the agenda will be set, and student outcomes are often discussed. The SUP will schedule a special meeting if he/she needs to discuss a major initiative in advance of a major decision.	Meeting agendas are set well in advance and often feature a presentation related to the school district's improvement agenda. SC members ask thoughtful questions to assist with the problem-solving. Difficult decisions are often discussed in informal public meetings (workshops, retreats, etc.) well before votes. The SC and SUP work together to include the community in major decisions, and make use of task forces and other joint committees to explore options.

	1	2	3	4
Monitoring	The SC is only aware of the district's progress in student outcomes when the SUP informs them. The data that is presented is limited or random and there is no clarity about which data or measures should be a priority.	The SC and the SUP review state test scores once a year as well as data that individual members may be interested in, but there is little sense how these numbers connect to district improvement initiatives and the SC has few means for holding the SUP accountable for student outcomes.	The SC and SUP periodically review student outcome data when working on the budget or at evaluation time. There is general agreement on what data is important to track.	The SC and SUP have agreed on a set of measures to judge the success of the superintendent's strategy and other goals the community has for its students. These are made easily assessable in a "data dashboard" or similar means, and meeting agendas are planned to periodically review data and to discuss progress. When the time comes to evaluate the SUP, the SC has a clear sense on what has been accomplished and what has not, and why.
Community engagement	Decisions are made in a vacuum. There is no public comment period, public engagement, or other opportunity for the community members and stakeholders to engage the SC. There is little or no interest in feedback from others.	The SC has authorized strategies for feedback, including public forums, public comment periods, and/ or district surveys. Policies on public input are clear and accessible and the Web site is generally up-to-date with meeting dates, agendas, and minutes. Communication, however, is primarily one-way.	The SC uses stakeholder feedback to inform budget, policy, and planning. Regular avenues for communication are scheduled, promoted and conducted in a way to encourage public input and follow-up, especially around big decisions.	The community expects and appreciates that the SC will engage stakeholders and other citizens in discussion and in search of feedback prior to making important decisions. There is a communication plan or policy, and the district enjoys a positive image in the community. Stakeholders may be asked to participate in focus groups or forums or on ad-hoc subcommittees from time to time.

Source: District Governance Support Project, Massachusetts Association of School Committees

In Workshop 2, we took the high road, so to speak, by emphasizing the special role of the school board in determining the long-range goals of the district. As elected representatives of the residents and parents of the locality, a school board is charged with overseeing the district. If they abandon this role, there is no one else who can do it, as the Panasonic Foundation has rightly pointed out. The new educator evaluation system put a focus on annual goals, but how would those be derived? The aim of Workshop 2 was to make sure that the board and superintendent team had a common understanding of what we began to refer to as the *overarching goals* of the district and how annual SMART goals and any other improvement plans would be consistent with that understanding.

If the district had not yet established long-term goals, coaches would take the concerns expressed by members and the superintendent at the end of Workshop 1 and group them into three or four common themes. During the workshop, members would work together to draft a goal statement for each theme. As the work product for this workshop, members decide how they will refine the goal statements prior to the next workshop. A final task of Workshop 2 gives members a chance to reflect on the results of the governance rubric.

Workshop 3: The Systems

Setting goals is a critical task of a school board; equally critical is deciding how to monitor progress toward the goals. After finalizing the overarching goals for the district, the third workshop is devoted to teasing out the types of data and other evidence that both the superintendent and committee agree will be tracked in order to monitor progress toward the agreed-upon goals. Together, participants brainstorm at least three presentations that could be given by the superintendent and staff during the year to monitor progress. Coaches introduce the concept of planning a yearlong agenda to schedule regular presentations on progress toward one or more goals. Participants assign the task of drafting such an agenda to one or more members as the work product for this workshop.

Workshop 4: The Walls

The goal of this workshop is to engage members in activities designed to make school board meetings more effective (i.e., focused on district goals), and helpful for members and the community at large. In pairs, the group undertakes an *agenda audit*, analyzing a year's worth of meeting agendas to reflect on whether the focus was on the *big bones* of student outcomes or *little bones* relating more to administrative matters. Members discuss the ideas of creating a data dashboard to keep the big picture of the district in mind; practicing the art of asking good questions about strategies and obstacles (as opposed to being a rubber-stamp or micromanaging board); and discussing their format preferences for meeting presentations. They also begin drafting guidelines for staff presentations as the work product for this session.

Workshop 5: The Roof

This workshop provides tools to sustain the committee's newly established practices in the future. The committee (and the superintendent) apply the governance rubric for a final time, and the coach scores and compares the results to the initial results from Workshop 1. This helps the group see where there has been progress and what areas could be tackled in future retreats. Work products completed during the previous four workshops are assembled into a draft handbook that can be used to recruit members, for new member orientations, and for helping the community better understand the roles of the school committee and superintendent. Committee members discuss ways that they can use their protocols to do regular board self-evaluations as part of the year-long agenda.

EVALUATING WHAT WORKED

Based on a case study of the program's success in Leominster, evaluators from the University of Massachusetts Donahue Institute identified six keys to successful implementation of the DGSP:

1. Determine that a majority of board members are willing to change and commit to the program.
2. Involve the superintendent as much as possible.
3. Proactively communicate with key constituencies.
4. Employ a knowledgeable coach with whom you enjoy working.

5. Take advantage of complimentary support programs that may already be in place.
6. Have a plan for continued success in order to ensure that new policies and practices remain intact through changes in leadership and/or committee membership.

In their final evaluation, evaluators encouraged the further refinements. Among other suggestions, they recommended that MASC develop a cadre of skilled coaches with deep familiarity with the training materials and with experience delivering them effectively. They recommended that MASC communicate expectations that the curriculum content and sequence of the workshops is important to achieving the desired program outcomes while maintaining some flexibility to adapt to district-specific needs and interests. Finally, they recommended that MASC consider bringing participating committees together, especially committee chairs, either in person or virtually to provide a chance for committees to learn from each other and share successful strategies.

Feedback from Participants

In interviews with a sampling of superintendents and committee chairs, participants said they valued the program in strikingly similar ways. Most said the fact that the project provided dedicated time for informal conversation about how to work together, to discuss roles and responsibilities, and to put the agreed-upon ways of working into written documents for future reference was especially valuable and helpful. One member noted, "We're working together better than before because of all those mornings we spent together." Having models of norms from other communities helped give their committee perspective on their roles as members, he said. As a result, "We are 'chewing on the big bones,' not creating more drama or peppering the staff with needless requests for more information."

"The protocols and things we were able to put in writing—those were the most useful things," said another participating member. "We had to have someone come in from the outside and show us that there is another way to operate; we could not have done that on our own . . . To have the [DGSP and NSIP] coaches working together on the superintendent piece, educating us about the roles and responsibilities of the superintendent, was very important. It's very, very easy to fall back into that micromanaging thing. We needed experienced experts to say, 'No, this is what you are supposed to be doing.'" Participants indicated that because of the program, the topics and conversation at meetings had become much more focused on goals relating to student outcomes, and several mentioned that they believed the community saw the committee in a more favorable light because of this.

In addition, two NSIP coaches said the program had helped new superintendents feel more confident in their relationship with their school committees. One coach, reflecting on the experience working with one new superintendent and his committee, said that

> the program was successful because it got them on the same page, with the same language and the same goals and the same desired outcome, so that they were able to work through conflicts, because the conflicts were rooted in style and the different perspectives that people brought with them. It let them define the obstacles as misunderstandings that could be worked through.

This coach pointed to the fact that the committee subsequently extended the superintendent's initial three-year term for an additional five years.

Participants also identified some of the challenges for the project in the future, including providing incentives for committees that are reluctant to *buy in* to the program and commit to the time necessary to complete all five workshops; more explicit training for board chairs in facilitation and in how to communicate with the superintendent and other members in times of crisis; and the ongoing challenge of continuing the work of revising norms regularly, especially after every election.

LOOKING AHEAD

In December 2013, federal and state support of the DGSP ended. As of this writing, more than forty districts have completed one or all of the DGSP workshops, and MASC is at work refining the DGSP as a membership service, with delivery to be provided—at least initially—by its field representatives on staff. Dorothy was hired as a full-time coordinator of the DGSP at MASC in the spring of 2014. In addition to recruiting districts to participate in future DSGP workshops, Dorothy is assisting leaders in the NSIP program to design a special stand-alone workshop to introduce the DGSP content for all new superintendents and their committees in Massachusetts.

Keeping the program current with the needs of districts is critical to its continued success. Changes that have occurred since the program's inception have already altered some of the workshops. Workshop 2 focuses on the creation of overarching goals. However, as the program expands, there are a growing number of districts that already have some version of overarching goals in place. For these committees, the discussion in Workshop 2 focuses more on the committee's role in realizing those goals. In addition to monitoring progress, committees discuss specific actions they must take, within their purview, to make progress on the overarching goals. Frequently, this discussion results in the creation of specific and measurable school committee goals in the areas related to budget, policy or community engagement.

The new state model for superintendent evaluations, which requires superintendents to create a portfolio of evidence has changed the discussion on creating dashboards as a monitoring tool in Workshop 4. Rather, committees and superintendents discuss what evidence will be presented during the course of the evaluation cycle to allow for the continuous monitoring of progress throughout the year. This discussion has proven valuable in the evaluation and monitoring process because it helps ensure that everyone is viewing goals and progress through the same lens.

While no in-depth study of DGSP's impact on student outcomes has yet been done, the authors believe that the responses from the initial participating districts strongly suggest its potential for helping local school boards create the conditions necessary for improved student achievement originally identified in the Lighthouse study and in subsequent studies referenced in this volume. Initial responses also indicate the potential for helping local school boards to find a Balanced Governance approach through agreed-upon processes that help them set overarching goals for the district and—through continuing conversations woven into regularly scheduled meetings—achieve a deep understanding of what is needed to accomplish these goals, while maintaining a respect for the specialized role of the superintendent as a partner in the process.

11

Lighthouse School Boards

Effective Boards Making an Impact on Student Achievement

CONNECTICUT LIGHTHOUSE STORY: *"YOU'RE CHANGING OUR CULTURE!"*

Nicholas D. Caruso Jr. and Warren Logee

In January 2009, a team of three people from Connecticut flew to Des Moines, Iowa, joining representatives of six other states to begin training with the Iowa Association of School Boards (IASB) in the Lighthouse board of education training model. The Connecticut team consisted of two consultants from the Connecticut State Department of Education (CSDE) and one trainer from the Connecticut Association of Boards of Education (CABE). In its annual allotment of funds to CABE, the CSDE provided seed money to begin the training that preliminary research showed could fill a void for training Connecticut boards of education. This partnership between CSDE and CABE continues to be a strength for Connecticut's Lighthouse program.

The Connecticut team was pleased to learn that the research upon which the Lighthouse project is based, the materials within the program, and the fundamental philosophies were similar to those already established by the CSDE in its work with Connecticut's lowest functioning school districts. The seven conditions of success, identified through research, that are found in high achieving districts, form a framework that can be used to bridge the critical achievement gaps that exist in some of the largest school districts in Connecticut. By (1) working together across the system, (2) knowing what it takes to change achievement, (3) providing workplace support, (4) providing professional development, (5) creating a balance between districtwide direction and building-level autonomy through extensive use of data, (6) building a strong community connection, and (7) distributing leadership, boards of education can focus their energies on the primary function of schools: providing high-quality instruction so that every child can learn at the maximum of his or her potential. The research also identified specific beliefs that must exist at high levels to improve achievement.

The original Lighthouse research project[1] included two surveys related to conditions and beliefs that serve as a benchmark for measuring the quality of Lighthouse training. The surveys are given to board members, administrators, and teachers annually to assess the progress the board is making toward improving those conditions and beliefs. The multistate team has restructured the survey to make it easier to complete. In Connecticut, we went a step further and commissioned a database and reporting system that allows us to delve more deeply into the survey results. The enhanced system allows boards to have a clearer understanding of the work that needs to be done.

In Connecticut, board members are typically from a business or political background and can be unfamiliar with issues related to teaching and learning. Frequently, board agendas reflect time spent on financial and personnel issues—items that are more familiar to board members or with which they have more experience (e.g., the "3 B's"—buildings, budgets, and buses). Lighthouse helps boards focus on leadership for improving student achievement and fosters increased and effective collaboration between superintendents and their boards.

By July 2009, after several trips to Iowa, one session in Chicago, and numerous planning sessions among the team, the Connecticut Lighthouse team was ready to begin offering the Lighthouse experience to Connecticut Boards of Education. The first board was from a small, economically disadvantaged community in a former industrial region of the state. Both the board and superintendent felt the program would help the board clarify beliefs about what is possible for student achievement in their community. In an effort to streamline the process and make efficient use of board members' time, the team decided to try to condense the first two training modules into one. That was a BIG MISTAKE!

The training structure consists of a series of modules, each designed to cover specific topics identified through Lighthouse research. The first module is critical for boards to understand the urgency surrounding the need for change to achieve their goals and what is at stake if they don't do anything. They must understand the board and the district must be a well-oiled machine working toward the same goals. We learned that in combining *Urgency* and *What's Possible* we failed to make the points as powerfully as needed, and the importance of the seven conditions was lost on the board members at first. A remarkable thing happened at the end of the session, however. The board chair acknowledged, "You are changing our culture." We felt exhilarated that in a brief time we had communicated enough of the philosophy that he could see the potential for the work we would do together. After two sessions they decided it would be beneficial to have district and building administrators participate in future meetings, and together they gained a new respect for the roles each must play; an obvious sense of trust was developed.

In another district it became apparent the community and board did not have a sense of *urgent* needs, as their state test achievement levels were high, and we mutually agreed to suspend the training after four sessions. The board chair and superintendent later reported that because of even our limited involvement, board meetings consisted of significantly more focused time on student achievement, and budget deliberations improved as members recognized the high priority for professional development necessary to maintain and enhance quality instruction.

Many training sessions provided *aha!* moments, both for the trainers and the trainees. In one district, board members struggled with identifying major roadblocks to improving student achievement. Using the book *Our Iceberg Is Melting*[2] as the basis for the Change Module, the team urged the board to think of the roadblocks as their iceberg. The board was able to identify that their iceberg is "a pervasive culture of low expectations" on the part of the community. This awareness helped them focus on their need to assume a strong leadership role to assert their commitment to improved student outcomes. The board committed to become strong advocates in the community to overcome the identified roadblock/iceberg. This led them to begin reviewing key policies to ensure that the policies were accurately reflecting the board's beliefs and expectations. A work session followed, which showed that most of the district's major policy statements did not mention student achievement. Because of this, the board has continued a complete policy review. Through the revised policies, the board is communicating their expectations for high student achievement throughout the district.

In several districts, the Connecticut Lighthouse team encountered significant challenges from which we learned much. In Connecticut's lowest performing district, officials at the State Department of Education mandated board participation in the Lighthouse process. The team felt that forcing a board to participate in Lighthouse would negatively affect the desired outcome. Representatives from the team met with the superintendent and key board members to reassure them that we all had the same agenda—the improvement of student learning. After an introductory presentation to the entire board, they voted unanimously to participate in the training, and several sessions were presented with full board participation. They were making progress until there was a change in district leadership and the board lost momentum.

In another district, the superintendent and board chair believed that Lighthouse training could bring a spirit of collaboration to a long-standing, strongly divided partisan board. It didn't have the desired effect and training sessions frequently degenerated into partisan bickering. The Lighthouse team, with agreement from the board chair and superintendent, made the decision to end the training.

Another of the low performing districts requested to participate in Lighthouse training, hoping the training would change the perception that the board and superintendent had a dysfunctional relationship. Several training modules were presented, but the members of the board showed little inclination to focus on issues related to improving student achievement. We started off on the wrong foot when the superintendent left the meeting just as we started the first module. As we stated earlier, we feel this is the most important session if the board-superintendent team is really going to gain from Lighthouse training. Lighthouse training was discontinued when the CSDE implemented more directive supervision of the board and district.

The team has found hesitation from superintendents who were concerned about role delineation between boards of education and administrators. In a district in which the superintendent was especially concerned over this issue before training began, he became a strong supporter when he saw that Lighthouse emphasized supporting the role of the superintendent, while strengthening the role that only the board can play in leading the district to high achievement for all students. Furthermore, the board came to understand more fully the good work the district was already doing to improve instruction.

Requiring attendance for two years of monthly meetings has proven to be more than most board members can sustain. The Connecticut Lighthouse team has worked to streamline the training program, while maintaining the integrity of the Lighthouse research and its essential components. We found that board members tend to stay the course over a one-year period. Following the presentation of essential modules, and firmly establishing the importance of the seven conditions found in effective school districts, the team has designed training to address specific district needs. Follow-up work is developed collaboratively by the Lighthouse team, the board, and the superintendent. Thus, the Connecticut training is personalized to meet a district's needs.

A renewed focus on keeping trainees actively involved in their own learning process throughout the training has led to training sessions in which trainees do more of the talking during small group work and reporting out to the larger group. In planning each session, trainers ask the question, "Is the group doing most of the work with the trainers facilitating that work?" The team has learned that some boards that work collaboratively and effectively during training, have difficulty relating Lighthouse learning to actions at board meetings.

It has become clear that the Lighthouse process is not designed to fix boards that are dysfunctional or that hold personal or political agendas as more important than collaborative effort to improve a school district's student outcomes. Boards of education and superintendents must be willing to work together to improve student achievement. When boards of education reach the point where they collectively want to be part of real school improvement, Lighthouse provides a vehicle for helping lead that change. In one of our Lighthouse districts, we were pleased to have the board enthusiastically tell us how they had applied their learning to their work at the board table as each training session started. That was not unique.

Our development of the training modules is always a work-in-progress because every board is different. We learn and improve our presentations with each training session. In particular, the Lighthouse data show that one of the weakest of the seven conditions in every district is *a strong community connection*. Every board we work with reinforces that community involvement and support are major challenges for their district. The Connecticut Lighthouse team continues to incorporate concepts that help boards identify their beliefs relative to community involvement and work to engage the community in meaningful ways.

We have spent countless hours, over six years, with this work. The preparation and planning for each training session, and the hands-on experience of the training sessions themselves, have led the team to believe this is some of the most rewarding and satisfying work in our long careers.

OREGON'S LIGHTHOUSE STORY

Renee Sessler

The Oregon School Boards Association (OSBA) began training three school boards in Lighthouse curriculum in 2009. One was located on the Oregon coast with approximately 4,000 students in two elementary schools, a middle school, a high school, an elementary charter school, a technology charter school for grades 6–12, and an online K–12 school. Another board was from a suburban district near Portland with a student population around 20,000 in twenty-five elementary schools, four middle and four high schools, plus three alternative schools. The third was right off Interstate 5 in southern Oregon with approximately 1,400 students in three elementary schools, one middle school, and one high school. All three school boards had seven members.

Each board received two years of Lighthouse training in 2009 to 2011 from one primary trainer and one policy specialist. They each approached the training a bit differently. The coastal district began training with only the board and superintendent participating, but included the building principals after a few sessions. The suburban district included the superintendent's cabinet from the district office, along with the board secretary, board, and superintendent; however, building principals did not participate. The southern school district included all the building principals, a teacher on special assignment (TOSA), and the board secretary along with the board and superintendent throughout the training. Each board experienced some turnover in membership during those two years with no negative consequence on the boards' learning.

When school districts include building principals in Lighthouse training from the beginning, the message penetrates deep within the school system. Therefore, when a board starts setting expectations for the school system, the leadership knows why and works more readily to meet those expectations. Building principals have stopped the trainer after sessions to share how they could have gone to other districts or retired, but with the Lighthouse training, they knew the school board was focusing on what really mattered, student learning, and they were so glad they stayed in their districts. This was the case for the southern school district, too, and why the rest of the Oregon story will be focused on the transformation there.

Distributing Leadership and Establishing Shared Priorities

Central to Lighthouse training is for school boards to understand and support distributed leadership throughout the district. The southern district board took the learning on distributed leadership to heart, directing the superintendent to assemble a team of teacher leaders from each building as well as all the building administrators and the TOSA to begin the work of improving student learning. Coinciding with the Lighthouse training, the superintendent worked with teachers and administrators to establish the district's priorities: "See each child; Make and keep the promise that all will succeed; Don't run alone, use the power of collaboration." The district also developed guiding questions:

- What is essential for each child to learn?
- How will we know they have learned what is essential?
- What will we do when they haven't learned what is essential?
- What will we do when they have learned what is essential?

All district staff members were made aware of these priorities and guiding questions, and each teacher was expected to determine and put in writing what is absolutely essential for their students to learn for each subject and grade level taught. Teachers worked in collaborative groups, initially within their own building and then later across grade levels throughout the district schools. Approximately one year into Lighthouse training, district administration selected key teacher leaders to participate in a Lighthouse training session with the board to share samples of their developing essential outcomes.

Common Assessments and Collaborative Data Studies for Monitoring Progress

During the second year of Lighthouse training, teachers were expected to develop common formative assessments to answer the guiding question "How will we know they have learned what is essential?" The teacher leaders were invited to another Lighthouse training session to share progress with the board on the development of common formative assessments and help the board develop a monitoring plan to review student learning data. To this day, teachers track all kinds of student learning data and the superintendent brings aspects of it to the board at its regular monthly business meetings. It is what the district calls the "How are the children?" portion of the meeting.

In addition to the monthly data reviews, the southern district board meets twice yearly with a district-level distributed leadership team (DLT) to analyze data on student learning. The first of these is in October when the board reviews student achievement data from the state's summative assessment and other available external data. Before that meeting, the board receives a data preview session with the superintendent and TOSA in September to prepare board members to ask questions of the DLT. During the October meeting, table groups are comprised of a board member, teacher leaders, and administrators to allow for in-depth conversations about the data. "The board members are really good about questioning without threatening," says the superintendent. "The board is good at gentle accountability, keeping pressure on the system with appropriate support."

The board always debriefs at a regular business meeting after the board-DLT meetings. Near the end of one board-DLT meeting, role groups met to discuss what they learned from the others, report out, and suggest what could improve the next meeting. The superintendent reported that the board's comfort level speaking together about student achievement is so great that at the report-out time, they wanted to keep talking about what they heard and what it means. The superintendent states, "They get so excited around what we're doing. It's a board that's come from not being immersed in education because they're outside education to being really comfortable talking about education and how we can make our school system better for our kids. The board has totally bought into the focus on student learning." The TOSA adds that when he was a classroom teacher he couldn't name any board member, didn't know them if he saw them, and there was a universal fear of the board among the teachers. Now the teachers are comfortable working with the board. The TOSA reports, "When board members are in our buildings, teachers know they are there to support."

In the middle of the school year, there are two more board-DLT meetings, one with elementary and the other with secondary, "just so we can handle the volume of data," says the superintendent. When the board reviews data it looks for trends, outliers, and patterns prompting the members to ask probing questions. If the board feels that meaningful information is missing, it asks that it be included in future review sessions. As teachers and administrators prepare for these sessions with the board, they are asked to think about how the board can use the data effectively. "Our board members are so well versed in the student achievement side of what we're doing and ask really good questions," reports the superintendent. Questions such as "How do you create your formative assessments?," "What kind of interventions are you using?," or "How do we know the essential outcomes are rigorous enough?"—those kinds of questions reverberate throughout the system and are talked about by teachers in every building.

Recently, such questions resulted in a restructuring of the district's use of professional learning groups. The secondary groups were initially in vertical groups (grades 9–12) by subject area and now are also in horizontal cross-discipline groups by grade level to determine consistency of essential outcomes between subjects. The elementary groups were already horizontal and now are vertical as well, to ensure that what is essential builds on each of the prior years' outcomes.

Balancing Districtwide Direction with Building-Level Autonomy

The district has a directive that staff answer all four of the guiding questions. There is not an option not to answer the questions; however, this directive is balanced with autonomy at the building level to determine how to go about answering the guiding questions. For example, one of the district's elementary schools established a system of ungraded primary grouping. Students move through subject areas on their own timeline and move in and out of groups with ease throughout the school year. A portion of the school retained traditional grade groups in conjunction with the ungraded groups. There was some concern by the other elementary schools that they would all be forced to adopt that model because it is one that the board liked and saw value in. However, even though the board is firm that all schools must ensure that students are learning the essential outcomes and making progress, a building will not be forced to adopt a particular practice unless that building chooses to do so.

Collaborative, Ongoing Study of Effects and Adjusting Actions

One of the intents of Lighthouse training is for boards to examine their practice in respect to how it affects student achievement and make changes to those practices that don't result in increased learning. The southern district superintendent reports, "Every summer we try to incorporate the board's roles and responsibility into our policy. And we have a board-superintendent working agreement. Annually, we review that working agreement so we know how we're working together." This conversation about how the board and superintendent each did over the past year gives them both comfort to operate as partners. The superintendent does not fear micromanagement by the board when invited as a student achievement partner, and the board respects the superintendent's unique role. Each party shares how the other did over the past year, and if one were to step out of line there is freedom to address that boundary violation right away. "It's a lot of work, but the board is very committed to it."

When asked if there were policy changes because of Lighthouse, the superintendent shared that the district's priorities—"See each child; Make and keep the promise that all will succeed; and Don't run alone, use the power of collaboration"—have been embedded in policy. The district's guiding questions, the essential outcomes it expects, and the board roles and responsibilities as identified in Lighthouse are also incorporated into policy. Another area of policy change is in the district's retention–social promotion processes to place each individual child into the best learning environment.

The superintendent believes the southern school board would sustain this system and interaction with a DLT should he move on to another district. This focus on the student achievement aspect of board work is now embedded in the culture and would continue. "Should the board ever need to hire another superintendent, it would hire one that agrees to work in this kind of a system." The board recognizes that this type of work requires more meetings, but values it and won't ever return to its former practice. In this district, the board has had little turnover since the training because of its members' commitment to the work. "The board is doing nice work, not micromanaging things, providing support where needed and meeting with the leadership team twice a year. Lots of ideas that came out of Lighthouse are still progressing and growing," says the TOSA.

Oregon Boards Showing the Way

In 2012 and 2013, seven more Oregon school boards began Lighthouse training, and initial results are promising, with other boards deciding to begin in 2014 and 2015. The sense of urgency for student learning to increase is spreading throughout participating districts and communities. Boards are practicing a Balanced Governance approach by learning together and figuring out how to fulfill their leadership roles to increase student learning. Board business meeting conversations are changing with more emphasis on student achievement. Leadership is being distributed, and board work sessions include key district leaders sharing data and helping board members know what is needed for higher student achievement. Teachers are recognizing that the board is serious about improving student learning and wanting to support their work so that all students can learn at high levels. *Lighthouses* are often found along ocean coasts to warn ships away from danger. In Oregon, Lighthouse school boards are beacons of hope found all throughout the state.

CONCLUSION

School Boards Matter for
Student Achievement

Phil Gore

The Fordham Institute got it right: "The fact that board members can influence achievement, even loosely, merits much more attention—surely by scholars but also by voters, parents, taxpayers, and other policy-makers."[1] In *Improving School Board Effectiveness: A Balanced Governance Approach*, we set out to describe current research that discusses how school boards can make a difference in student outcomes. We have also offered practical tools and examples of promising practices. We sincerely hope that board members, administrators, and those seeking to study and support school governance find this book to be a valuable resource for improvement and a catalyst for further research.

While historically there has been a lack of board involvement in issues related to student achievement, diligent board members today seek to clearly understand and fulfill their leadership role to govern for improved student achievement. As this book makes clear, the research tells us that school boards make a difference in student achievement. Their values and beliefs,[2] actions,[3] teamwork,[4] and turnover[5] all influence learning and teaching. As Alsbury states in the introduction, "When the structures and norms of behavior within the school culture positively affect instructional practices, improved student achievement is expected and typical."

Today, we know more than ever about the actions and processes of school boards that associate with improved student learning. As Lorentzen identified from his research and the Washington State School Board Standards, highly functioning school boards

- model responsible school district governance by working as an effective and collaborative team;
- hold the school district accountable for meeting student-learning expectations by evaluating the superintendent on clear and focused expectations;
- set and communicate high expectations for student learning with clear goals and plans for meeting those expectations;
- commit to a continuous improvement plan regarding student achievement at each school and throughout the district;
- provide responsible school district governance by conducting board and district business in a fair, respectful, and responsible manner;
- engage the local community and represent the values and expectations the community holds for its schools; and
- create districtwide conditions for student and staff success.

DESCRIBING BALANCED GOVERNANCE

As emphasized in the introduction to this book, Balanced Governance is not a narrow approach to fixing one area of board practice or dealing with a problem board member. Balanced Governance is a mindset and a framework for informed and intentional school governance. In these pages, we have shared purposeful board practices, informed by research, that thoughtful board members and superintendents can adapt and apply in their unique settings.

As a researcher, director of board training and development, and a former school board member, I approach this work with a conviction that publicly elected school governance is not broken but rather needs improvement. As we have seen, a commitment to and focus on improving student achievement is critical for effective school governance. The primary message in these pages acknowledges a need for improved student achievement while suggesting that a balanced perspective and approach are the best way to get there. We know from biology and systems theory that nature loves a balance. Machines function optimally and human beings are most healthy and successful when systems are in balance. We are encouraging a similar balance in matters of school governance and improvement. This requires intentional leadership by the individual school board members and superintendents that make up a district's governance team.

Balanced Governance is not a single prescribed model or program, but describes an approach that finds balance between overprescription and willful ignorance. Highly capable boards are knowledgeable and thoughtful about what it takes to improve student learning. They are eager to support administrators who lead with vision to achieve a reality of all students achieving at high levels. Capable board members strive to become cheerleaders for successful schools and programs, *and* they demand that their districts develop and maintain successful schools and programs.

Balanced Governance supports neither uninformed delegation nor micromanagement. In this approach, board members hold the superintendent accountable for reporting on progress and demonstrating that the district is improving. Board members stay informed of the needs of the district and ask clarifying questions that support their understanding for decision making. They do not engage in suggesting which program to use or try to guide implementation, but they do ask informed questions, so they can both support and evaluate progress.

As stated in the introduction, most high achieving boards function in a balanced governance paradigm whether or not they use the term. We think of Balanced Governance as a descriptor of values, beliefs, and actions that we observe in high functioning school boards. We believe that the practical examples of board training programs, standards, assessments, and recommendations from highly effective boards in this book are valuable to board members, superintendents, and researchers committed to improving public education.

Responsibility of Governance

Balanced Governance supports board members operating within a framework that resonates with responsible and civic-minded citizens. Our intent throughout the development of this book has been to equip, prepare, support, and encourage highly effective school board service. A keen awareness of the responsibility of school boards and their members undergirds the examples and suggestions.

The overwhelming majority of school board members and superintendents are responsible citizens striving for excellence of outcomes for the students in their district. Improving the achievement of all students is the responsibility of every person working in public education. It is imperative that school boards and their members set aside petty differences and preferences and govern their districts in the most effective manner that builds public trust and support, and more importantly, provides equitable and high achievement for all students. This requires leadership.

Leadership Through Governance

School boards are at the intersection of public policy and public school administration. As such, they can play a pivotal role for ensuring that student achievement is high and equitable as well as consistent with the vision their communities have for their schools. Importantly, school boards and their members can also play a significant role in helping to lead and shape the vision that the community has for its schools. When board members lead in pursuit of equitable and high achievement, all of us benefit.

Publicly elected school board members and the superintendents they hire are well positioned to provide the leadership necessary for improvement. This leadership hinges on an ongoing conversation focused consistently on student learning. This conversation among the board and with the superintendent requires clear communication, commitment to equity, and an unwavering commitment to do whatever it takes to improve outcomes for children.

Balanced Governance board members engage with the community in ways that build confidence and involvement in the school district. Because board members want to serve their communities, they often have diverse ties to community members and other stakeholders. Those ties enable them to represent a collective vision that their community has for its schools. They typically bring a large amount of social capital that they can leverage to expand community partnerships that enhance opportunities for students.

A HERITAGE TO IMPROVE

We believe democratically elected school boards are an American heritage that needs support for continued success. Our nation's founders were strategic and thoughtful when they chose to entrust state and local citizens with the governance of our schools. This heritage is a gift to be improved, not a fleeting effort to abolish. Improvement will come, and does come, when actors apply themselves to the pursuit of excellence. No specific training or pathway adequately prepares someone for the complexities of school board service. On the other hand, every time one engages in civil discourse, considers what constitutes an equitable process or outcome, or participates in public service, she or he is preparing for effective school board service.

The vast majority of school board members serve for the greater good of their communities, state, and nation. When asked why they joined their local school board, overwhelmingly board members cite that they want to give something back. We frequently hear that they are thankful for the public education they received. Board members appreciate the opportunities that public education afforded them and their children, and they want to ensure that other children have the same opportunities that they had—or better. Many refer to school board service as a calling, an honor, and a responsibility. Personally, when offered the opportunity to join our city council, my reply to our mayor was, "It seems like the school board would be a more natural place for me to serve our community."

Alsbury articulated in chapter 7 that not just the board as a whole matters, but individual board members also affect the stability and continuity of school improvement. Veteran superintendents can attest to how challenging one or two board members can make their work and affect the progress and continuity of the school system. At the same time, a strength of democratic selection can be increased perspectives and diversity of opinion. How board members, together with a superintendent, mitigate challenges of personalities that operate independently of the whole board could be the subject of an additional book. However, the term *balance* could apply well in those situations.

Board-Superintendent Relationships

Throughout this book we highlight the importance of the relationship between an elected citizen school board and a hired superintendent as a critical factor in student success. This intersection of democratically elected lay citizens and hired professional administrators represents a pivotal opportunity for district outcomes. It behooves each conscientious board member and superintendent to strive to make this relationship and the critical work of the governance team a success. Improving superintendent evaluation is one key opportunity for improving success of the school district. Making evaluation a clear and agreed process from the beginning of the cycle and a conversation about growth and district performance is a critical factor in the board-superintendent relationship. Again, this requires an application of Balanced Governance that is intentional and thought through in advance.

Applying a Balanced Governance mindset and approach requires reflective practice by school board members. When board members apply a basic continuous improvement model to their individual practice—*Plan, Do, Check, Act*—they are likely to find themselves acting toward the middle of the Balanced Governance continuum. That is, most of the time. There can be times when a reflective and intentional board member will move toward the micromanagement end of the spectrum. This can result from information that suggests something unethical or illegal might be happening. It might appropriately occur when a superintendent provides insufficient data or supporting evidence for decision making. One highly capable board member stated, "I trust the superintendent and support him fully, but if I sense something may be covered up or the story is incomplete, I'm going down." While reflective board members that are striving for Balanced Governance may be inclined *not* to micromanage, capable superintendents will stay attuned to the need for information and can help board members avoid this situation.

This is an issue rarely if ever discussed in school governance literature. Superintendents need to be reminded not to encourage micromanagement and not to micromanage their board. If a superintendent asks one time for board members' opinions on things like bus schedules, paint colors, and personnel actions, it becomes difficult for board members not to offer their opinions when those types of items arise in the future. Similarly, if a superintendent models micromanagement by telling board members how to think about and vote on issues, board members will be more likely to replicate that behavior toward the superintendent.

Stabilizing the Tension

There is no one-size-fits-all solution for governing the approximately 13,000 public school districts in the United States. Likewise, there is no cure-all approach that works in every interaction of board members and their superintendents. Wise and capable superintendents may prefer a little micromanagement by board members to disengagement and apathy. Like other human phenomena, this can be a difficult dance between control and disengagement. The fact remains, however, that while the board-superintendent relationship may sometimes be delicate, it is critical to the outcomes of the district.

Alsbury's stabilizing characteristics provide a powerful reflective tool for intentional board practice. Board members and superintendents alike would do well to engage in regular self-examination, asking themselves whether they are practicing these stabilizing characteristics in their interactions with each other and community stakeholders. The resounding concept here is that reflective, intentional practice is a key for growth and improvement. As the governance team models learning and improvement, this sets the tone for the expectations of students and staff throughout the school system.

RECOGNITION AND AN INVITATION

We are deeply grateful for each author and contributor to the chapters in this book. We are equally grateful for the readers of this book. This has been a long-time discussion and journey for Thomas Alsbury and me to review and collect contributions from dedicated researchers and practitioners and share those with you. We look forward to hearing and seeing how these concepts are applied and expanded to improve public school governance. We invite you to collaborate with us in ongoing research and school governance improvement efforts. Please share your perspectives and challenges with us. Thank you in advance for partnering with us to provide increased scrutiny of and support for the influence of school boards on student achievement. In the end, it really is all about the kids—*each and every one of them.*

NOTES

Foreword

1. Arnold F. Shober and Michael T. Hartney, *Does School Board Leadership Matter?* (Washington, DC: Thomas B. Fordham Institute, 2014), 4.
2. Willard R. Daggett, *The Daggett System for Effective Instruction: Alignment for Student Achievement* (Rexford, NY: International Center for Leadership in Education, 2014), http://www.leadered.com/pdf/Daggett_System_for_Effective_Instruction_2014.pdf.

Introduction

1. Mary L. Delagardelle, "The Lighthouse Inquiry: Examining the Role of School Board Leadership in the Improvement of Student Achievement," in *The Future of School Board Governance: Relevancy and Revelation*, ed. Thomas L. Alsbury (Lanham, MD: Rowman and Littlefield, 2008), 191–224.
2. Steven A. Petersen, "Board of Education Involvement in School Decisions and Student Achievement," *Public Administration Quarterly* 24, no. 1: 46–68.
3. Argun Saatcioglu and Gokce Sargut, "Sociology of School Boards: A Social Capital Perspective," *Sociological Inquiry* 84: 42–74.
4. Thomas L. Alsbury, "School Board Politics and Student Achievement," in *The Future of School Board Governance*, 247–272.
5. Alsbury, *The Future of School Board Governance*.
6. William G. Howell, *Besieged: School Boards and the Future of Education Politics* (Washington, DC: Brookings Institute Press, 2005).
7. Nancy Walser, *The Essential School Board Book: Better Governance in the Age of Accountability* (Cambridge, MA: Harvard Education Press, 2009).
8. Arnold F. Shober and Michael T. Hartney, *Does School Board Leadership Matter?* (Washington, DC: Thomas B. Fordham Institute, 2014).
9. Quoted in Frederick M. Hess and Olivia Meeks, *School Boards Circa 2010: Governance in the Accountability Era* (Washington, DC: Thomas B. Fordham Institute, 2010), 5.
10. Kenneth K. Wong and Francis X. Shen, "Education Mayors and Big-City School Boards: New Directions, New Evidence," in *The Future of School Board Governance*, 319–356; Thomas L. Alsbury, "Should the K–12 organizational structure of schools in the U.S. be changed dramatically?" in *Debating Issues in American* Education, eds. Charles J. Russo and Allan G. Osborne Jr. (Thousand Oaks, CA: Sage, 2011), vol. 7, 245–264; Diane Ravitch, "*USA Today* Gets It Wrong on Mayoral Control of Schools," *Huffington Post*, March 23, 2007, http://www.huffingtonpost.com/diane-ravitch/usa-today-gets-it-wrong-o_b_44104.html.

11. OECD, "Lessons from PISA 2012 for the United States: Strong Performers and Success-ful Reformers in Education," http://dx.doi.org/10.1787/9789264207585-en.

12. Howell, *Besieged*.

13. Laurence Iannaccone and Frank W. Lutz, "The Crucible of Democracy: The Local Arena," *Journal of Educational Policy* 71, no. 5: 39–52.

14. Alsbury, *The Future of School Board Governance*.

15. Andrew A. Lipscomb and Albert E. Bergh, *The Writings of Thomas Jefferson* (Washington, DC: Thomas Jefferson Memorial Association of the United States, 1853–1854).

16. Alsbury, *The Future of School Board Governance*.

Chapter 1

1. Ellen Henderson, Jeannie Henry, Judith B. Saks, and Anne Wright, *Team Leadership for Student Achievement: The Roles of the School Board and the Superintendent* (Alexandria, VA: National School Board Association, 2001).

2. Thomas L. Alsbury, ed., *The Future of School Board Governance: Relevancy and Revelation* (Lanham, MD: Rowman and Littlefield, 2008); Peter Coleman and Linda LaRocque, *Struggling to Be Good Enough: Administrative Practices and School District Ethos* (Basingstoke, NH: Falmer Press, 1990); Mary L. Delagardelle, "The Lighthouse Inquiry: Examining the Role of School Board Leadership in the Improvement of Student Achievement," in *The Future of School Board Governance*, Alsbury, 191–224; Mary L. Delagardelle, "Roles and Responsibilities of Local School Board Members in Relation to Student Achievement" (doctoral thesis, Iowa State University, 2006).

3. Bruce Joyce, Mary L. Delagardelle, and Jim Wolf, "The Lighthouse Inquiry: School Board/Superintendent Team Behaviors in School Districts with Extreme Differences in Student Achievement" (paper presented at the annual meeting of the American Educational Research Association, Seattle, WA, Apr. 10, 2001); Delagardelle, "Lighthouse Inquiry," 191–224.

4. Frederick M. Hess and Olivia Meeks, *School Boards Circa 2010: Governance in the Account-ability Era* (Arlington, VA: National School Boards Association, the Thomas Fordham Institute, and the Iowa School Boards Foundation, 2010).

5. Arnold F. Shober and Michael T. Hartney, *Does School Board Leadership Matter?* (Washington, DC: Thomas B. Fordham Institute, 2014).

6. Delagardelle, "Lighthouse Inquiry."

7. Hess and Meeks, *School Boards Circa 2010*.

8. Joyce, Delagardelle, and Wolf, "Lighthouse Inquiry."

9. Hess and Meeks, *School Boards Circa 2010*.

10. Richard F. Elmore, *Building a New Structure for School Leadership* (Washington, DC: Albert Shanker Institute, 2000).

Chapter 2

1. Thomas L. Alsbury, "School Board Member and Superintendent Turnover and the Influ-ence on Student Achievement: An Application of the Dissatisfaction Theory," *Leadership and Policy in Schools* 7, no. 2 (2008a): 202–229.

2. Ibid.; Thomas L. Alsbury, ed., *The Future of School Board Governance: Relevancy and Reve-lation* (Blue Ridge Summit, PA: Rowman and Littlefield Education, 2008b); Deborah

Land, "Local School Boards Under Review," *Review of Educational Research* 72 (2002): 229–278.

3. Michael A. Resnick, *Effective School Governance: A Look at Today's Practice and Tomorrow's Promise* (Denver, CO: Education Commission of the States, 1999).

4. Alsbury, *Future of School Board Governance*; Thomas L. Alsbury, "Does School Board Turnover Matter? Revisiting Critical Variables in the Dissatisfaction Theory of American Democracy," *International Journal of Leadership in Education* 7, no. 4 (2004): 357–377; Theodore J. Kowalski, *The School Superintendent: Theory, Practice, and Cases*, 2nd ed. (Thousand Oaks, CA: Sage, 2006).

5. Land, "Local School Boards Under Review."

6. Richard H. Goodman, Luann Fulbright, and William G. Zimmerman, *Getting There from Here. School Board-Superintendent Collaboration: Creating a School Governance Team Capable of Raising Student Achievement* (Arlington, VA: Educational Research Service, 1997); Richard H. Goodman, Luann Fulbright, and William G. Zimmerman, *Thinking Differently: Recommendations for 21st Century School Board/Superintendent Leadership, Governance, and Teamwork for High Student Achievement* (Arlington, VA: Educational Research Service, 2000).

7. Iowa Association of School Boards, "IASB's Lighthouse Study: School Boards and Student Achievement," *Iowa School Board Compass* 5, no. 2 (2000): 1–12; Iowa Association of School Boards, *Leadership for Student Learning: The School Board's Role in Creating School Districts Where All Students Succeed* (Des Moines, IA: IASB, 2007).

8. Iowa Association of School Boards, *Leadership for Student Learning*.

9. Martha A. MacIver and Elizabeth Farley-Ripple, *Bringing the District Back In: The Role of the Central Office in Instruction and Achievement* (Alexandria, VA: Educational Research Service, 2008).

10. Timothy Waters and Robert J. Marzano, "School District Leadership that Works: The Effect of Superintendent Leadership on Student Achievement," *ERS Spectrum* 25, no. 2 (2007): 1–12.

11. Goodman, Fulbright, and Zimmerman, *Thinking Differently*.

12. Larry Lashway, *Using School Board Policy to Improve Student Achievement* (Eugene, OR: ERIC Clearinghouse on Educational Management, 2012).

13. Goodman, Fulbright, and Zimmerman, *Getting There from Here*.

14. Gordon Cawelti and Nancy Protheroe, *High Student Achievement: How Six School Districts Changed into High-Performance Systems* (Arlington, VA: Educational Research Service, 2001).

15. Thomas Shelton, "The Effects of School System Superintendents, School Boards and their Interactions on Longitudinal Measures of Districts' Students' Mathematics Achievement" (PhD dissertation, University of Louisville, 2010).

16. Iowa Association of School Boards, "IASB's Lighthouse Study."

17. Alsbury, "School Board Member and Superintendent Turnover."

18. Ibid.

Chapter 3

1. John E. Chubb and Terry M. Moe, *Politics, Markets, and America's Schools* (Washington, DC: Brookings Institution, 1990).

2. Frederick M. Wirt and Michael W. Kirst, *The Political Dynamics of American Education*, 3rd ed. (Berkeley, CA: McCutchan, 2001).
3. Iowa Association of School Boards,"IASB's Lighthouse Study: School Boards and Student Achievement," *Iowa School Board Compass* 5, no. 2 (2000): 1–12; Thomas L. Alsbury, "School Board Politics and Student Achievement," in *The Future of School Board Governance: Relevancy and Revelation*, ed. Thomas L. Alsbury (Lanham, MD: Rowman and Littlefield, 2008), 247–272; Gene I. Maeroff, *School Boards in America: A Flawed Exercise in Democracy* (New York: Palgrave Macmillan, 2010); Argun Saatcioglu, Suzanne Moore, Gokce Sargut, and Aarti Bajaj, "The Role of School Board Social Capital in District Governance: Effects on Financial and Academic Outcomes," *Leadership and Policy in Schools* 10 (2010): 1–42; Ivan J. Lorentzen, "The Relationship Between School Board Governance Behaviors and Student Achievement" (doctoral dissertation, University of Montana, 2013).
4. Argun Saatcioglu and Gokce Sargut, "Sociology of School Boards: A Social Capital Perspective," *Sociological Inquiry* 84 (2014): 42–74.
5. Ronald S. Burt, *Brokerage and Closure: An Introduction to Social Capital* (New York: Oxford University Press, 2005).
6. Thomas L. Alsbury, "Superintendent and School Board Member Turnover: Political versus Apolitical Turnover as a Critical Variable in the Application of the Dissatisfaction Theory," *Educational Administration Quarterly* 39 (2003): 667–698; Theodore J. Kowalski, "The Future of Local District Governance: Implications for Board Members and Superintendents," in *Advances in Research and Theories of School Management and Educational Policy*, vol. 6: *The New Superintendency*, eds. Cryss C. Brunner and Lars G. Bjork (New York: JAI Press, 2001), 183–203.
7. Douglas E. Mitchell and Garu W. Badarak, "Political Ideology and School Board Politics," *Urban Education* 12, (1977): 55–83.
8. Meredith Mountford, "Historical and Current Tensions Among Board-Superintendent Teams: Symptoms or Cause?" in *The Future of School Board Governance*, Alsbury, 81–114.
9. Norman D. Kerr, "The School Board As an Agency of Legitimation," *Sociology of Education* 38 (1964): 34–59.
10. Jonathan C. Wilson, "Urban Education: A Board Member's Perspective," *Phi Delta Kappan* 75 (1994): 382–386.
11. Laurence Iannaccone and Frank W. Lutz, "The Crucible of Democracy: The Local Arena," *Politics of Education Association Yearbook* 9 (1994): 39–52.
12. Robert D. Putnam, Robert Leonardi, Raffaella Nanetti, and Franco Pavoncello, "Examining Institutional Success: The Case of Italian Regional Government," *American Political Science Review* 77 (1983): 55–74.
13. Janine Nahapiet and Sumantra Goshal, "Social Capital, Intellectual Capital, and the Organizational Advantage," *Academy of Management Review* 23 (1998): 242–266.
14. Brian Uzzi, "The Sources and Consequences of Embeddedness for the Economic Performance of Organizations: The Network Effect," *American Sociological Review* 61: 674–698.
15. Burt, *Brokerage and Closure*; David Krackhardt, "Social Networks," in *Encyclopedia of Group Processes and Intergroup Relations*, ed. John M. Levine and Michael A. Hogg (Los Angeles: Sage Publications, 2010), 817–821.

16. Jeffrey Pfeffer and Gerald Salancik, *The External Control of Organizations* (New York: Harper and Row, 1978).

17. William L. Boyd, *Competing Models of Schools and Communities: The Struggle to Reframe and Reinvent Their Relationships* (Philadelphia: National Research Center on Education in the Inner Cities, 1996); Bonnie C. Fusarelli, "The Politics of Coordinated Services for Children: Interinstitutional Services and Social Justice," in *Handbook of Education Politics and Policy*, ed. Bruce S. Cooper, John G. Cibulka, and Lance D. Fusarelli (New York: Routledge, 2008), 350–373.

18. Barbara Lau, *Public Involvement, Public Education, Public Benefit* (Washington, DC: Public Education Network and Education Week, 2004).

19. Peter C. Scales, Karen C. Foster, Marc Mannes, Megan A. Horst, Kristina C. Pinto, and Audra Rutherford, "School-Business Partnerships, Developmental Assets, and Positive Outcomes among Urban High School Students," *Urban Education* 40 (2005): 144–189.

20. Roberta Tracthman, "School/Business Collaborations: A Study of the Process and Product" (doctoral dissertation, Hofstra University, 2013).

21. Katherine L. Hughes, Thomas R. Bailey, and Melinda J. Mechur, *School-to-Work: Making a Difference in Education* (New York: Institute on Education and the Economy, Teachers College, Columbia University, 2002).

22. Burt, *Brokerage and Closure*.

23. AnnaLee Saxenian, *Regional Advantage: Culture and Competition in Silicon Valley and Route 128* (Cambridge, MA: Harvard University Press, 1994).

24. Keith Provan and H. Brinton Milward, "A Preliminary Theory of Interorganizational Network Effectiveness: A Comparative Study of Four Community Mental Health Systems," *Administrative Science Quarterly* 40 (1995): 1–33.

25. Deborah G. Ancona and David F. Caldwell, "Bridging the Boundary: External Activity and Performance in Organizational Teams," *Administrative Science Quarterly* 37 (1992): 634–651; Ray E. Reagans and Ezra W. Zuckerman, "Networks, Diversity, and Productivity: The Social Capital of Corporate R&D Teams," *Organization Science* 12 (2001): 502–517.

26. Iowa Association of School Boards, "IASB's Lighthouse Study: School Boards and Student Achievement," *Iowa School Board Compass* 5, no. 2 (2000).

27. Thomas L. Alsbury, "School Board Member and Superintendent Turnover and the Influence on Student Achievement: An Application of the Dissatisfaction Theory," *Leadership and Policy in Schools* 7 (2008): 202–229; Alsbury, "School Board Politics and Student Achievement."

28. Saatcioglu, Moore, Sargut, and Bajaj, "The Role of School Board Social Capital"; Saatcioglu and Sargut, "Sociology of School Boards."

29. Paul S. Adler and Seok-Woo Kwon, "Social Capital: Prospects for a New Concept," *Academy of Management Review* 27 (2002): 17–40.

30. Carrie R. Leana and Frits K. Pil, "Social Capital and Organizational Performance: Evidence from Urban Public Schools," *Organization Science* 17 (2006): 353–366.

31. Deborah Land, "Local School Boards Under Review: Their Role and Effectiveness in Relation to Students' Academic Achievement," *Review of Educational Research* 72 (2002): 229–278.

Chapter 4

1. George Maeroff, *School Boards in America: A Flawed Exercise in Democracy* (New York: Palgrave Macmillian, 2010), 15.
2. American Association of School Administrators, "What Is the Goal of Public Education?" *The Leader's Edge*, Sept. 2004.
3. Mary L. Delagardelle, "The Lighthouse Inquiry: Examining the Role of School Board Leadership in the Improvement of Student Achievement," in *The Future of School Board Governance: Relevancy and Revelation*, ed. Thomas L. Alsbury (Lanham, MD: Rowman and Littlefield, 2008), 191–223; Nancy Walser, *The Essential School Board Book: Better Governance in the Age of Accountability* (Cambridge, MA: Harvard Education Press, 2009).
4. Ivan J. Lorentzen, "The Relationship Between School Board Governance Behaviors and Student Achievement Scores" (doctoral dissertation, University of Montana, 2013).
5. Thomas L. Alsbury, "School Board Politics and Student Achievement," in *The Future of School Board Governance*, 247–272; Delagardelle, "Lighthouse Inquiry"; Lorentzen, "Relationship Between School Board Governance."
6. Alsbury, "School Board Politics and Student Achievement"; Nicholas D. Caruso, "Teach the Board its Proper Role," *School Administrator* 62, no. 9 (2005); Richard H. Goodman and William G. Zimmerman Jr., *Thinking Differently: Recommendations for 21st Century School Board/Superintendent Leadership, Governance, and Teamwork for High Student Achievement* (Arlington, VA: Educational Research Service, 2000); Frederick M. Hess and Olivia Meeks, *Governance in the Accountability Era: School Boards Circa 2010* (National School Boards Association, The Thomas B. Fordham Institute, and The Iowa School Boards Foundation, 2010) http://files.eric.ed.gov/fulltext/ED515849.pdf; Walser, "Essential School Board Book."
7. Washington State School Directors' Association, *Washington School Board Standards, Benchmarks of Success and Indicators for Evaluation: With References.* June, 2009, http://www.wssda.org/Portals/0/Resources/Publications/standardsdetailed.pdf, 1.
8. Goodman and Zimmerman, *Thinking Differently*; Washington State School Directors' Association, 2009.
9. J. Timothy Waters and Robert J. Marzano, "School District Leadership That Works: The Effect of Superintendent Leadership on Student Achievement. A Working Paper" (Denver, CO: McREL, Sept. 2006), http://files.eric.ed.gov/fulltext/ED494270.pdf.
10. Delagardelle, "Lighthouse Inquiry."
11. Katheryn W. Gemberling, Carl W. Smith, and Joseph S. Villani, *The Key Works of School Boards: A Guidebook* (Alexandria, VA: National School Boards Association, 2000).
12. Washington State School Directors' Association, 2009.
13. Lorentzen, "Relationship Between School Board Governance."
14. Ibid.
15. Ibid.
16. Steven A. Peterson, "Board of Education involvement in school decisions and student achievement," *Public Administration Quarterly* 24, no. 1 (2000): 46–68.
17. Washington State School Directors' Association, 2009.
18. Goodman and Zimmerman, *Thinking Differently*, 17.

19. For example, see Andrew Calkins, William Guenther, Grace Belfore, and Dave Lash, *The Turnaround Challenge: Why America's Best Opportunity to Dramatically Improve Student Achievement Lies in our Worst-Performing Schools* (Boston, MA: Mass Insight Education and Research Institute, 2007); Julie Kowal, Emily Ayscue Hassel, and Bryan C. Hassel, *Successful School Turnarounds: Seven Steps for District Leaders* (Washington, DC: The Center for Comprehensive School Reform and Improvement, 2009); and Ronald C. Brady, *Can Failing Schools Be Fixed?* (Washington, DC: The Fordham Foundation, 2003).

20. Paul Houston, "Superintendents for the 21st Century: It's Not Just a Job, It's a Calling," *Phi Delta Kappan* 82 (2001): 429–433.

21. Lorentzen, "Relationship Between School Board Governance."

22. Thomas L. Alsbury, "School Board Member and Superintendent Turnover and the Influence on Student Achievement: An Application of the Dissatisfaction Theory," *Leadership and Policy in Schools* 7 (2008): 202–229.

23. Matthew M. Chingos, Grover J. (Russ) Whitehurst, and Katharine M. Lindquist, *School Superintendents: Vital or Irrelevant?* (Washington, DC: Brookings Institution, Sept. 2014), 1.

Chapter 5

1. Thomas L. Alsbury, ed., *The Future of School Board Governance: Relevancy and Revelation* (Lanham, MD: Rowman and Littlefield, 2008), 247–272; Mary L. Delagardelle, "The Lighthouse Inquiry: Examining the Role of School Board Leadership in the Improvement of Student Achievement," in *The Future of School Board Governance*, Alsbury, 191–223; Deborah Land, "Local School Boards Under Review: Their Role and Effectiveness in Relation to Students' Academic Achievement," *Review of Educational Research* 72 (2002): 229–278.

2. Larry Lashway, "Using Board Policy to Improve Student Achievement," *ERIC Digest*, 2002: 163, ERIC No. ED472183-2002-12-00.

3. Frederick M. Hess and Olivia Meeks, *Governance in the Accountability Era: School Boards Circa 2010* (National School Boards Association, The Thomas B. Fordham Institute and the Iowa School Board Foundation, 2010); Land, "Local School Boards Under Review."

4. Alsbury, *Future of School Board Governance*; Delagardelle, "Lighthouse Inquiry."

5. Land, "Local School Boards Under Review."

6. Delagardelle, "Lighthouse Inquiry."

7. Nancy Walser, *The Essential School Board Book: Better Governance in the Age of Accountability* (Cambridge, MA: Harvard Education Press, 2009).

8. Mark Levine and Thomas L. Alsbury, "The Role of School Boards in Governance, Leadership & Educational Reform in Maryland" (paper presented at the annual meeting of the American Educational Research Association, Philadelphia, April 3–7, 2014).

9. Wendy E. Ruona, *An Investigation into Core Beliefs Underlying the Profession of Human Resource Development* (St. Paul, MN: University of Minnesota, HRD Research Center, 1999); Richard A. Swanson and David E. Arnold, "The Purpose of Human Resource Development Is to Improve Organizational Performance," in *Workplace Learning: Debating the Future of Educating Adults in the Workplace*, ed. R. W. Rowden (San Francisco: Jossey-Bass, 1996), 13–20.

10. Linda Dawson and Randy Quinn, "A Board-Superintendent Relationship Based on De-fined Goals Can Raise Achievement," *The School Administrator* 61, no. 10 (2004).

11. Richard H. Goodman and William G. Zimmerman Jr., *Thinking Differently: Recommendations for 21st Century School Board/Superintendent Leadership, Governance, and Teamwork for High Student Achievement* (Arlington, VA: New England School Development Council and Educational Research Services, 2000, ERIC Record ED480398), 15.

12. Kathrine W. Gemberling, Carl W. Smith, and Joseph S. Villani, *The Key Work of School Boards Guidebook* (Alexandria, VA: National School Boards Association, 2000), 6.

13. Alsbury, *Future of School Board Governance*; Delagardelle, "Lighthouse Inquiry"; William Howell, *Besieged: School Boards and the Future of Education Politics* (Washington, DC: Brookings Institution Press, 2005); Walser, *Essential School Board Book*.

14. Terry Bevino, "Unfinished Business: An Analysis of the Turnaround of Okaloosa Schools 2001–2005 and a Roadmap for Doing Even Better" (report commissioned by the Okaloosa County, FL, school board) Sept. 12, 2005, http://www.okaloosaschools.com/files/school district/_docs/UnfinishedBusiness.pdf.

Chapter 6

1. Modified and used with permission by the Oregon Educational Investment Board: Equity Lens.

2. Kenneth Leithwood, Robert Aitken, and Doris Jantzi, *Making Schools Smarter: Leading With Evidence*, 3rd ed. (Thousand Oaks, CA: Corwin, 2006).

3. Richard P. DuFour and Robert Eaker, *Professional Learning Communities at Work: Best Practices for Enhancing Student Achievement* (Bloomington, IN: Solution Tree Press, 1998), 25.

4. Patrick Lencioni, *The Four Obsessions of an Extraordinary Executive* (San Francisco: Jossey-Bass, 2000), 153.

Chapter 7

1. Thomas L. Alsbury, "Does School Board Turnover Matter? Revisiting Critical Variables in the Dissatisfaction Theory of American Democracy," *International Journal of Leadership in Education* 7, no. 4 (2004): 357–377.

2. Laurence Iannaccone and Frank W. Lutz, "The Crucible of Democracy: The Local Arena," *Journal of Educational Policy* 9, no. 5 (1994): 39–52.

3. Laurence Iannaccone, "Callahan's Vulnerability Thesis and 'Dissatisfaction Theory,'" *Peabody Journal of Education* 71, no. 2 (1996): 110–119; Thomas L. Alsbury, "Superintendent and School Board Member Turnover: Political Versus Apolitical Turnover as a Critical Variable in the Application of the Dissatisfaction Theory," *Educational Administration Quarterly* 39, no. 5 (2003): 667–698.

4. Alsbury, "Does School Board Turnover Matter?"

5. Thomas L. Alsbury, "School Board Politics and Student Achievement," in *The Future of School Board Governance: Relevancy and Revelation*, ed. Thomas L. Alsbury (Lanham, MD: Rowman and Littlefield, 2008), 247–272.

6. Theodore J. Kowalski, "School Reform, Civic Engagement, and School Board Leadership," in *The Future of School Board Governance*, Alsbury, 312–339.

7. Terry L. Cooper, Thomas A. Bryer, and Jack W. Meek, "Citizen-Centered Collaborative Public Management," *Public Administration Review* 66, no. s1 (2006): 76–88.
8. Argun Saatcioglu and Gokce Sargut, "Sociology of School Boards: A Social Capital Perspective," *Sociological Inquiry* 84 (2014): 42–74.
9. Stephen A. Peterson, "Board of Education Involvement in School Decisions and Student Achievement," *Public Administration Quarterly* 24, no. 1 (2000): 46–68.

Chapter 8

1. Ivan J. Lorentzen, "The Relationship Between School Board Governance Behaviors and Student Achievement Scores" (doctoral dissertation, University of Montana, 2013).
2. Phil Gore, "A Deeper Look at Superintendent Evaluation: A Framework and Process for Improvement" (presentation at the annual conference of the National School Board Association, New Orleans, April 4, 2014).
3. Frederick M. Hess and Olivia Meeks, *Governance in the Accountability Era: School Boards Circa 2010* (National School Boards Association, The Thomas B. Fordham Institute and the Iowa School Board Foundation, 2010).
4. Ann Allen and Michael Mintrom, "Responsibility and School Governance," *Educational Policy* 24, no. 4 (2010): 439–464.
5. Terry M. Moe, "The Two Democratic Purposes of Public Education," in *Rediscovering the Democratic Purposes of Education*, eds. Lorraine M. McDonnell, P. Michael Timpane, and Roger Benjamin (Lawrence, KS: University Press of Kansas, 2000).
6. Jim Thomas, *Doing Critical Ethnography* (Newbury Park, CA: Sage, 1993).
7. David Labaree, "Public Goods, Private Goods: The American Struggle Over Education Goals," *American Educational Research Journal* 34, no. 1 (1997): 39–81.
8. Margaret Plecki, Julie McCleery, and Michael Knapp, *Redefining and Improving School District Governance* (Seattle, WA: Center for the Study of Teaching and Learning, University of Washington, Oct. 2006).
9. Hess and Meeks, "Governance in the Accountability Era."
10. Gore, "A Deeper Look at Superintendent Evaluation."
11. Mary L. Delagardelle, "The Lighthouse Inquiry: Examining the Role of School Board Leadership in the Improvement of Student Achievement," in *The Future of School Board Governance: Relevancy and Revelation*, ed. Thomas L. Alsbury (Lanham, MD: Rowman and Littlefield, 2008), 191–223.
12. Argun Saatcioglu and Gokce Sargut, "Sociology of School Boards: A Social Capital Perspective," *Sociological Inquiry* 84:42–74.

Chapter 9

1. This chapter draws directly from an unpublished paper entitled "Doing the Right Thing: Guidance for Effective School Boards," which was written for the Panasonic Foundation by Patricia Mitchell, Andrew Gelber, Sophie Sa, and Scott Thompson.

Chapter 10

1. School boards in Massachusetts are called school committees.

2. See chapter 8 for a description of SMART goals.

Chapter 11

1. See chapter 1 for a description of the Lighthouse studies.
2. John Kotter and Holger Rathgeber, *Our Iceberg Is Melting: Changing and Succeeding Under Any Conditions* (New York: St. Martin's Press, 2005).

Conclusion

1. Arnold F. Shober and Michael T. Hartney, *Does School Board Leadership Matter?* (Washington, DC: Thomas B. Fordham Institute, 2014).
2. Mary L. Delagardelle, "The Lighthouse Inquiry: Examining the Role of School Board Leadership in the Improvement of Student Achievement," in *The Future of School Board Governance: Relevancy and Revelation*, ed. Thomas L. Alsbury (Lanham, MD: Rowman and Littlefield, 2008), 191–224.
3. Steven A. Petersen, "Board of Education Involvement in School Decisions and Student Achievement," *Public Administration Quarterly* 24, no. 1: 46–68.
4. Argun Saatcioglu and Gokce Sargut, "Sociology of School Boards: A Social Capital Perspective," *Sociological Inquiry* 84: 42–74.
5. Thomas L. Alsbury, "School Board Politics and Student Achievement," in *The Future of School Board Governance*, Alsbury, 247–272.

ACKNOWLEDGMENTS

We want to acknowledge the excellent assistance of the editorial staff at Harvard Education Press with special thanks to Nancy Walser, who initially encouraged the development of this book. We'd like to thank our colleagues and practitioners who contributed to the book chapters and who provided the important link between research and practice. Special thanks to the Connecticut Association of Boards of Education, Massachusetts Association of School Committees, Montana School Boards Association, Oregon School Boards Association, Texas Association of School Boards, Washington School Directors' Association, Panasonic Foundation, and National School Boards Association. We want to thank our wives and families for their ongoing support. Finally, we would like to thank all of the elected school board members, who serve day in and day out with little or no compensation, and more than their share of professional and personal criticism, in order to help our nation's children achieve their dreams.

ABOUT THE EDITORS

Thomas L. Alsbury is professor of educational leadership at Seattle Pacific University, and former school teacher, principal, and administrator. He also served as professor at Iowa State University and North Carolina State University. He currently co-directs the national University Council for Educational Administration (UCEA) Center for Research on the Superintendency and District Governance. Alsbury completed an M.Ed. in educational curriculum and instruction from the University of Washington and an Ed.D. in educational leadership and counseling psychology from Washington State University. Alsbury is listed as the foremost expert on school governance by the Associated Press; he has consulted on school governance issues in twelve countries and across the United States and is a frequent keynote speaker and presenter at school board state and national conferences and state association events. He has worked with local urban and rural school boards to evaluate and assist in improving performance. He has over fifty publications on school board and superintendent research. His 2008 book, *The Future of School Board Governance: Relevance and Revelation*, earned Dr. Alsbury the UCEA Culbertson Award for significant contributions to educational leadership research. Alsbury is also founder and president of Balanced Governance Solutions (www.balancedgovernancesolutions.org), an organization committed to the research, development, and training in effective school board governance.

Phil Gore, a former Seattle-area school board member, is the division director for leadership team services with the Texas Association of School Boards. He has worked with the National School Boards Association and was the Director of Leadership Development Services for the Washington School Directors' Association. During his time in Washington, Phil led a statewide initiative to develop multiple validated approaches and tools for superintendent evaluation in the state. Prior to working in school governance, Phil was a pastor and youth minister for twenty years. Phil is completing a PhD this year at the University of Washington in educational leadership and policy studies. His doctoral research focuses on the factors and sources of information that school boards consider when evaluating a superintendent. Phil has an M.Ed. in educational leadership and policy studies and a BA in management. When he is not assisting school boards and superintendents, Phil enjoys mountain climbing, kayaking, and long-distance running with his wife and children. Phil can be reached at goreph@gmail.com.

ABOUT THE CONTRIBUTORS

Nicholas D. Caruso Jr. is a former member of the Bloomfield (CT) board of education, serving from 1983 to 1993. During his tenure on the board he served as board secretary and board chair. While serving on the board, Nick also served on the board of directors for the Connecticut Association of Boards of Education, as chair of the State Relations Committee, and as the Association's first vice-president. He left the board in 1993 to become a lobbyist for the Connecticut Conference of Municipalities, working for local town governments, but soon found himself back at CABE as a staff member. Nick is responsible for board training and facilitation and the coordination of technology, as well as other tasks. He is a member of the National School Boards Association advisers group (seen regularly in the *American School Board Journal*) and a regular columnist (The Board Savvy Superintendent) for *School Administrator* magazine. Nick has had articles published in several national publications and has presented nationally on various topics. He also served on the steering committee for the Connecticut Partnership for 21st Century Schools and was a long-standing member of the board of directors for the Connecticut Academy for Education in Mathematics, Science and Technology. Nick represented CABE on the Joint Committee for Educational Technology. He currently serves on the Connecticut Commission for Educational Technology. Nick has had the pleasure to work with 149 of the 169 Connecticut boards of education, doing over a thousand workshops covering a variety of topics including basic roles and responsibilities, board evaluation, goal setting, and effective meetings. Nick is currently involved in the Lighthouse Project, a research-based training program designed to help boards of education focus on improving student achievement.

Mary L. Delagardelle is associate division director of the PK–12 Division of Learning and Results in the Iowa Department of Education and a former teacher, principal, central office administrator, and board member/board president in Iowa school districts. She has a BA in elementary education, an MA in special education, administrative certification, and a PhD in education with an emphasis on educational leadership and policy studies. In addition to her many years in public education, she also served as the deputy executive director of the Iowa Association of School Boards and the executive director of the Iowa School Boards Foundation, where she was the developer and director of the landmark Lighthouse Research Project throughout all phases of the study from 1998 through 2011. She has been an adjunct instructor for two of Iowa's state universities, teaching classes on school governance, board-superintendent relationships, and educational leadership. She has coordinated, led, and/or provided training for numerous schoolwide, districtwide, and statewide initiatives for improving school culture, improving content, improving the practice of teachers and administrators, and improving student learning outcomes. She has published works related to school boards, parent involvement, mathematics reform, and programming for students with special needs.

Andrew Gelber has been a senior consultant with the Panasonic Foundation since 1994. In that capacity he has worked with school boards, superintendents, teachers, and principals across a wide variety of school districts (including Boston; Atlanta; Denver; Norfolk, VA; Allentown, Lancaster, and Norristown, PA; Howard and Montgomery Counties, MD; and Elizabeth, NJ) on issues ranging from teacher and principal professional development to systemwide strategic planning to school board development. He has assisted school boards and superintendents with the development of tools and processes for superintendent evaluation and school board self-evaluation, and for improving communication between superintendent and school board. Prior to 1994, Andrew was director of school programs for PATHS/PRISM: The Philadelphia Partnership for Education. In that capacity, he designed and implemented a wide range of systemwide and school-based professional development programs for teachers and principals in the School District of Philadelphia, including a nationally recognized K–12 Writing Across the Curriculum initiative.

Mark Levine was an adjunct instructor for behavior management curriculum at Barry University and a behavior specialist for a Florida school district for ten years after serving in public and private educational leadership, administrative and human resource, and development roles for twenty years. Mark received his MA from Kent State and PhD in education and leadership, with a specialization in human resource development, from Barry University. While collaborating with state school board associations, Mark codeveloped the MHL© governance assessment instrument used in his research and coauthored several published studies on school board governance and student achievement.

Warren Logee has spent the last forty-two years as an educator in Connecticut. After teaching for eight years in Simsbury, he became an elementary school principal in Plainville. In 1978 Warren became principal at John F. Kennedy School in Windsor and remained in Windsor until retiring in 2003. While in Windsor, Warren's schools regularly demonstrated high academic achievement, with Education Trust recognizing Kennedy School in a 1998 study as a school with high minority population and high academic achievement.

Since leaving the Windsor public schools, Warren has worked as a consultant for CREC, the University of Connecticut, and, for the past five years, as a leader in residence at the Connecticut State Department of Education in the Bureau for Accountability and School Improvement. In the latter capacity, Mr. Logee was the lead consultant providing technical assistance in four of the fifteen original partner districts around data teams, district and school improvement plans, and accountability. In addition, Mr. Logee has been trained and delivers training, in partnership with the Connecticut Association of Boards of Education, in the Lighthouse Project that provides training for boards of education in its role in and accountability for improved student achievement. Throughout his career, Warren has delivered many workshops and presentations related to improving student achievement. He has trained teachers and administrators to improve school climate and culture. He also has worked with many groups to improve capacity to utilize data to drive instructional decisions and measure student progress on an ongoing basis.

Ivan J. Lorentzen is professor of psychology, and director of The Scholars Program, serving over forty years at Flathead Valley Community College in Kalispell, MT. He has served in elected positions on local elementary and high school boards for twenty years and was presented with the Marvin Heintz Award in 2010 for Outstanding Achievement as a School Trustee in Montana. He earned the Eagle Award at FVCC as outstanding college faculty member in 2002, and was recognized nationally by the Association of Community College Trustees as the Outstanding Faculty Member for the Western Region in 2012. In 2013 he completed a study in Montana on the relationship between boardsmanship and student achievement.

William P. McCaw has been a public school educator since 1979. His experience includes twenty years in P–12 education as a teacher, principal, and central office administrator. In 1999 Bill transitioned to the University of Montana-Missoula as a faculty member in the Department of Educational Leadership, working primarily with principal and superintendent candidates. His research focus examines the roles and relationships between school leaders and followers, and the development of personal and organizational environments conducive to optimal performance. Dr. McCaw has considerable experience in the theoretical and practical aspects of education reform; specifically in the areas of curriculum, supervision, assessment, and organizational behavior. Bill's work influences leadership policy at the state, national, and international levels.

Betsy Miller-Jones is executive director of the Oregon School Boards Association. She began her work in school board governance as a locally elected school board member in Londonderry, NH, in 1994. Betsy served as a board member in New Hampshire for six years and worked for the New Hampshire School Boards Association before moving to OSBA in 2004. She is a nationally recognized board trainer, presenting at the National School Boards Association annual conference and at other state conferences. Betsy redesigned OSBA's board development training plan, and has developed and presented workshops statewide on a variety of topics including board roles and responsibilities, goal setting and strategic planning, superintendent evaluation, and building a strong leadership team.

Under Betsy's leadership, OSBA has provided Lighthouse training to local school boards. Currently, as executive director, Betsy is committed to providing the best possible services to Oregon's school boards, so they may improve achievement for every student. Betsy has a BSE in engineering from Duke University and an MBA from the University of North Carolina at Chapel Hill.

Larry Nyland currently serves as superintendent of the Seattle public schools. He has also served as superintendent in several other school districts in Washington and Alaska. Larry is passionate about creating communities of caring, justice, and equity. He is known for bringing communities together around student learning and student success. Nyland earned a PhD in educational administration from the University of Washington and developed the superintendent preparation program while serving as associate professor at Seattle Pacific University. Larry has provided training and leadership development services to dozens of school boards and school districts. He was named as Washington superintendent of the year, and a national finalist with AASA, in 2007. His school board was selected as Washington board of the year in 2012. He is a former Kellogg Leadership Fellow and serves on the executive board for the Kellogg Fellows Leadership Alliance.

Dorothy Presser is a field director with the Massachusetts Association of School Committees and served as MASC president in 2011. Presser has served on the Lynnfield, MA, school committee since 1998, chairing the committee for twelve years of her tenure. She completed and was later a co-coordinator for the Institute for Educational Leadership's Education Policy Fellowship Program, a program for educational professionals focused on public policy and leadership skills. Presser also served as a curriculum design committee member and coach for the District Governance Support Project. In her role as field director, she continues to coach and to refine the project's curriculum, keeping it current with the needs of participating committees.

Argun Saatcioglu is associate professor of education and (by courtesy) sociology at the University of Kansas. He specializes in the sociology of organizations and sociology of education. His research interests include educational governance and policy evaluation and racial/ethnic stratification in K–12 schooling. His recent work has appeared in *Sociological Inquiry*; *American Journal of Education*; *Du Bois Review: Social Science Research on Race*; *Teachers College Record*; *Social Science History* and *Leadership and Policy in Schools*.

Renee Sessler is a former member of the Reynolds, OR, school district board of directors; serving from 1995 to 2004. During her service she served as both board chairman and vice chairman. While serving on that board, Renee also served on the board of directors for the Oregon School Boards Association and as trustee for both the health insurance and the property and casualty trusts. She left her school board service to pursue a career in school board professional development, first in Idaho and now in Oregon. Her work with the Lighthouse Project began in 2007.

Tom Shelton was Kentucky's 2011 superintendent of the year and is the executive director of the Kentucky Association of School Superintendents in Frankfort. He formerly served as the superintendent of Fayette County public schools in Lexington, and prior to that as the superintendent of Daviess County public schools in Owensboro. His dissertation, "The Effects of School System Superintendents, School Boards and Their Interactions on Longitudinal Measures of Districts' Students' Mathematics Achievement," won both the Districts in Research and Reform group's dissertation of the year award and the Research on the Superintendency group's dissertation of the year award from the American Education Research Association.

Scott Thompson is assistant executive director of the Panasonic Foundation, a corporate philanthropy devoted to the systemic improvement of public education in the United States, and the editor of *Strategies*, an issues series by the Panasonic Foundation in cooperation with the American Association of School Administrators and the University Council for Educational Administration. Thompson, who started his career as a high school English teacher, is author of *Leading from the Eye of the Storm* (Rowman and Littlefield Education, 2005), a book that illuminates the inner work of leading school systems through the complexities of full-scale, sustainable improvement. Prior to joining the staff of the Panasonic Foundation in

1996, Thompson was director of dissemination and project development at the Institute for Responsive Education and the editor of *New Schools, New Communities.*

Paul Van Buskirk was an adjunct professor for advanced statistics at Barry University and adjunct professor for statistics for planning analysis at Florida Gulf Coast University. Paul taught for several years at Rensselaer Polytechnic Institute, where he received his undergraduate degree in the engineering sciences. He has a PhD from Barry University in education and leadership with a specialization in human resource development. Paul is the recipient of the Charles Evans Hughes Award from the American Society of Public Administration for Outstanding Service in Public Administration and is the author of a book on the case study of comprehensive social, economic, and physical planning through community participation. He is a coauthor of several published studies in urban modeling, and as an experienced urban modeler developed a software program that assists communities and school districts to assess their planning and governance decisions. He has been designated a fellow at the New York State Academy of Public Administration.

Nancy Walser is editor of the *Harvard Education Letter* and an acquiring editor at the Harvard Education Press. A former newspaper journalist, Walser served eight years on the Cambridge school committee before stepping down to complete her M.Ed. in education policy and management from the Harvard Graduate School of Education. Her research on high functioning boards led to the publication of *The Essential School Board Book: Better Governance in the Age of Accountability* (Harvard Education Press), which was named one of the most notable education books of 2009 by the *American School Board Journal.* She is a frequent speaker and consultant on the subject of effective board practices. From 2010 to 2013 she served as a curriculum design committee member and coach for the District Governance Support Project described in chapter 10 of this book.

INDEX